Penelope Red

Consequences
Beyond
Belief

This edition first published in paperback by
Michael Terence Publishing in 2023
www.mtp.agency

Copyright © 2023 Penelope Red

Penelope Red has asserted the right to be identified as
the author of this work in accordance with the
Copyright, Designs and Patents Act 1988

ISBN 9781800945593

No part of this publication may be reproduced, stored
in a retrieval system, or transmitted, in any form or
by any means, electronic, mechanical, photocopying,
recording or otherwise, without the prior
permission of the publisher

Cover design
Copyright © 2023 Michael Terence Publishing

Michael Terence
Publishing

Foreword

To Lucas, you inspire me to be a better person every day - I would not be here without you. Thank you for being you.

To my family, who I hope never read this - "you can love your family as well as having family wounds".

To Mr M - Thank you for being a mentor, role model and friend to Lucas and me. We owe you.

- Penelope Xx -

Contents

Introduction 1

The Secret 4
Family Secrets & The Drug Trade 15
My Mother 22
My Mum's Parents
(The Irish One & The Unknown One) 44
My Father 49
My Nan 56
My Mum's Lover & My Step Dad 63
My Sister 72
My Uncles 78
The Misunderstood Child 82
Mental Health & My Diagnosis 90
Finding Love & Family 109
The Now 120

Appendix 136

Introduction

In my childhood, I never had anybody who had experienced anything I was experiencing, nor was there online tools/fact finding. I will go into this later on my aspirations and the motivation for writing this. But in essence I am hoping if I can get one person to read this and take something from it, whether it be the similarities or the differences from their own experiences then it is a success. So, strap in and prepare to question what you think you know about addiction.

Before I start, I do want to do some housekeeping and caution you for some trigger warnings. What we are covering in this book does cover addiction and mental health services which are hard hitting areas. I want to highlight some Helplines here so if you are reading any of these and feel affected by anything please reach out below:

- Emergencies Call 999
- Local Police Call 101
- Childline Call 0800 1111
- Samaritans Call 116 123
- SHOUT: Text SHOUT to 85258 for messaging services
- National Domestic Abuse Helpline Call 0808 2000 247
- The Mix (Under 25s) Call 0808 808 4994
- NACAO 0800 358 3456

Spoiler alert, my mum doesn't become clean and the world doesn't turn into rainbows and smell of roses, like being in a Lush store with overpriced bath bombs. I feel I've healed a lot of our wounds by talking to others, but I have only been able to get to this place by healing and finding myself, by going back in time to move forward.

Healing is a positive word, but healing isn't linear and can feel different hour to hour. Healing can feel positive, but it can also feel exciting, peaceful, worth it, confusing and mundane. You can often question the process and feel you are taking two steps back, so be kind to yourself and your journey. Ironically, when we start to get better, we start to realise how much we've missed out on, how badly certain people failed their obligation to us, and what the younger version of us actually deserved. Healing involves healthy grieving. No way around it. Again, grieving is not just for the loss of a loved one and I encourage you to look at the stages of grief as you are probably experiencing these.

My mum hasn't and will not change. And I believe this quote poetically puts this coming to some sort of peace. *"As traumatised children, we always dreamed that someone would come and save us, we never dreamed that it would be ourselves as adults"* Alice Little.

Every story is unique and deserves to be told. I've read a few stories that have made me physically cry and I think thank God I didn't have that, what have I got to complain about?

It was only until somebody said to me they feel they didn't deserve to moan about their family situation because of mine that I interjected and guess corrected myself in the process. Trauma is also unique. Trauma is not what happened to you, it is what happened inside of you.

There is always somebody who has had a worse experience than you. There is always somebody who has had a better experience than you. This doesn't mean you don't deserve to be heard. Your story makes you unique and however you feel your feelings are valid. Children of addicts & children of traumas big or small have a place and the availability to all the same services. Look after yourself. If you read this and feel you had a different experience, it doesn't make your experience any less valid. You did not deserve your trauma OR any trauma. Everyone has a place here. Just because someone else's events of trauma are your type of normal doesn't make it okay.

Whilst I know I am broken, there is common term used against broken people, that they know they can survive. We generally can get through anything. Sometimes I don't feel like that, but my past experiences show me different.

The Secret

My mum is a heroin addict. Commonly known as a 'junkie' or a 'smackhead'. God, that is crazy to write that. And no, she is not a Jeremy Kyle heroin addict. I didn't survive on benefits and live in a council house with no heating. You may have watched the film Trainspotting with Ewan McGregor and have an idea of what a heroin addict is, well buckle up, this is a new story. My mum was and still is a high functioning addict. *"High functioning drug addicts and alcoholics are people who have a substance use disorder but can still manage their day-to-day activities."* [1] She is a successful woman, dresses well, looks like she has got all of her ducks in a row. But I ask you this, can a heroin addict be a good mum, high functioning or not?

The fear of writing this is so scary. There are consequences for myself and my family that could come on the back of this, and it feels a constant battle and debate of should I write it, or shouldn't I. My life story is something that I hid, due to judgement, a view of pity and embarrassment, so laying it all down is a horrifying thought. How do I structure such a chaotic mess? Where do I begin? I am using this as a platform to express my past, my present and hopefully set the parameters for my future.

I have also spent hours and hours reading books and looking through people's life stories to almost understand it. And some things in life, you can google the answer, like what year did man land on the moon, but for addiction and family matters, it's an individual journey. For me the biggest lesson was childhood trauma does not only influence your emotional state but also your biological state. Your brain finds ways to adapt in each set

---

[1] https://www.renewallodge.com/are-you-a-high-functioning-drug-addict/

of circumstances we are handed. As per Dr Perry states in *What happened to you, Dr Bruce Perry & Oprah Winfrey*, "Understanding how the brain reacts to stress or early trauma, helps clarify how what has happened to us shapes who we are, how we behave and why we do the things we do."

My life is full of holding others' secrets. So much so I've started to pour out like a faulty watering can. My family all seem to have their secrets, and I was told them and had to own them from a young age. Even now, I think I want to know secrets, because I've always grown up being told things I maybe shouldn't know, so now I seek them out, and then once I know them I just carry the heavy burden. That is a character trait I need to improve on.

The comical thing in all of this, is that my mum worked as a social worker. Yes, the lady who would look like she had all her life together would come and judge you because you didn't work or let your dog shit on the floor next to where your baby was playing. She would come home and tell horror stories of babies being sat in dirty nappies all day, with us feeling so grateful we didn't have that. But we did have a pathological liar and a master of disguise.

Heroin. It's such a taboo word. I still to this day wish it was cocaine or alcohol addiction. At least people talk about that. All addiction is horrible and I do not wish any of them addictions on anyone, and this is in no way to say heroin is worse - but that is just how I felt at the time.

I went through a period of hanging out with drug dealers and even they wouldn't talk about it. When I would come home from school I would raid my mum's room for her stash. It may sound odd, but she would always lie and say she was off it, and unless I found it, I would believe her... 'cause she's still my mum the woman who carried me for 9 months, feeds me, keeps a roof over my head, doesn't let me go out with dirty clothes etc.

I would search everywhere, and she got better at hiding it. Like a squirrel hiding their prized nuts. She didn't hide the methadone bottles like the needles. My mum would just put them in the bathroom bin with the bloody tissues, or leave them in her dressing gown pocket. I still remember the green liquid within the brown bottles, I can still picture them in my mind. The bottles were sticky and when you held them it felt like the substance was seeping into your skin. They are quite cunning at hiding, which I have to give them credit for. Putting them in pillowcases, mattress' seams and just generally places you didn't think would be possible. I would search with fear, however, as I was aware I could be pricked by one of them if I did find it and I really didn't want to be injected, but my need for the truth outweighed the risk. Even now, I still feel that way.

Do you know the symptoms of heroin abuse? And no not just the stereotypes of homelessness, drowsiness but the actual symptoms to look out for? I know these nearly off by heart, data from themanorclinic.com:

- Constricted pupils (My mum always has tiny pupils, I always try to look at them whenever I see her and always compare to other peoples, as I want to make sure it's not just the light)
- Uncontrollable itching (my mum has eczema, like me so I always would excuse this, but it was always her arms around her vein area, as well as she would always bleed from her and constantly wear long sleeves)
- Respiratory Problems (my mum has had asthma all her life, so this can also be hid through her asthma)
- Persistent flu like symptoms
- Regular chest infections (she'd get these like I got a common cold)
- Watery eyes and runny nose

- Gastrointestinal problems (she has had operations for her gallbladder twice, not sure if these are connected)
- Constipated
- Scabs, bruises, scratches, sores or other skin damage due to injecting heroin
- Disrupted sleep patterns
- Malnutrition
- Unintentional, significant weight loss
- Exhaustion
- Pneumonia and tuberculosis
- Kidney & Liver disease
- Hepatitis C, HIV/AIDS as a result of sharing infected needles
- Infection of the heart lining and valve
- Seizures
- Bloods clots
- Loss of menstrual cycle in women

As you can see there is a lot here, and some I would argue are more caused by heroin use than symptoms of diseases. But even so, as I discuss with my mum's near-death experience, there are some diseases missing from this list too and some unknown risks of heroin addiction. I find it interesting that nothing on mental health is on there either.

I've only just recently found out when she started using. It was when I was an innocent one-year-old. She had just separated from my father and had two young kids and didn't know what else to do. At least I'm not a smack baby - right? But the question I always ask myself is why wasn't I enough? Was the pressure of having a second child too much? Did my existence split my parents up and drive my mum to drugs?

So finding out the secret is a bit of a blur. I always knew something was up. Sometimes my mum and step dad would just be knocked out for the whole day, like zombies. I now know it's because that was when they couldn't access the drugs if their supplier was short or something, or if they overdosed themselves or got arrested. But my older sister and I would have to go through the day without any food, no help, or nothing. We did call our dad once but my mum rang him and said we were being dramatic. Why didn't she let him take us? A big part of her recovery is admitting we were in the way of her drug taking, and she's admitted that to us, which isn't the nicest. But why didn't she let us go? Why did she continue to hide and lie to everyone?

The thing with heroin is that nobody really knows a lot about it. Like I've said earlier it is a taboo. We are all ignorant of it. We know they inject it. Think it's green. If you pictured a heroin addict you would think gutter level. My mum also took methadone which if you look online basically says is a death sentence to take the combination. "Since heroin is a short-acting narcotic, people could mix heroin and methadone to draw out the high and take the edge off comedown effects when heroin begins to leave the person's body. The mixture could be intended to enhance the high from heroin by adding a second narcotic sedative; this does not create the same potent high as mixing benzodiazepines or alcohol with methadone, but it can still cause a high that can lead to overdose." [2]

I have spent a lot of time researching heroin, for obvious reasons, because it is so unknown and a secretive world. Heroin is a type of opioid. "Opioids are a class of drugs naturally found in the opium poppy plant and that work in the brain to produce a variety of effects, including the relief of pain with many of these

---

[2] https://americanaddictioncenters.org/methadone-addiction/and-mixing-heroin

drugs."[3] Did you know in America every 25 minutes a baby is born with opioid withdrawals? That shook me to my core. A lot of people with opioid addiction are prescribed pain killers in which they become addicted. However my mum's 'prescription' sadly wasn't even legal, which made me not able to speak to anyone about it even further.

All addictions are as severe, and may have different symptoms but the damage they do to the taker and their close circle are normally quite similar. You see a lot about cocaine, alcohol and gambling addiction in the media. Especially in the current age, too, I think cocaine has become a bit of an epidemic. According to the Office for National Statistics England & Wales, There were 840 deaths involving cocaine registered in 2021, which was 8.1% higher than the previous year (777 deaths) and more than seven times higher than in 2011 (112 deaths). I know a lot of people around my age who take cocaine as if it were a glass of wine and would do it while going to their local pub on a Saturday. But opioids don't seem to have the research or discussion around it like the other addictions. I am in no way suggesting that it deserves a bigger platform, but an equal one. How many of you knew heroin was from a plant?

I am also so scared of becoming a mother, because there is a horrifying thought of what if I turn out like mine? Or what if my mum poisons my child? But also, I don't think I have the strength to stop my mum seeing my child because I know she will love it, but that won't stop her being high around them, like it didn't stop her with me as a baby. Imagine depriving your mother of being a grandparent, because she would spoil them materialistically and I am convinced she would love them, but is that also unfair on the children?

---

[3] https://www.hopkinsmedicine.org/health/treatment-tests-and-therapies/opioids

You might be thinking, are you being dramatic? But the question is constantly asked around is addiction hereditary? Is it genetics? We all know a lot of addicts have come through growing up around addicted family/friends, so is it nature vs nurture? The American Psychological Association (APA) claims that "at least half of a person's susceptibility to drug or alcohol addiction can be linked to genetic factors".

This question could also be linked to how do we stop the cycle of abused becoming the abuser? We've all seen the documentaries. We've all seen the films where someone behaves a certain way and the penny drops when they reveal what a terrible childhood they had. Sometimes they even clutch at this to explain behaviour, for example recently watching the John Wayne Gacy tapes on Netflix and they tried to 'defend' his behaviour due to his strict father. Or in the case of Ted Bundy, who seemingly had a normal upbringing, psychologists and behaviourists still struggle to understand why he did what he did as he had no childhood trauma to generate the evil feelings and actions he did.

I am in no way linking normal people to the very sparse number of serial killers and murderers, but these are what we see in the media a lot linked with dysfunctional pasts. Now we all know most people don't end up like that, but they do end up becoming an abuser themself. Take my mum, she had a difficult childhood and was beaten by my step dad, and she became my abuser in terms of a negligent parent, rather than turning that experience and making sure she doesn't abuse anyone due to her experience. And some people do, like myself, I want to reinvent that wheel.

It is really difficult to sit here and say my mum and step dad didn't have difficult lives, and their drug taking and abuse has come from certain reasons. I have spoken with a few psychologists and they link the abused becoming the abuser, and others are linked with suppressed anger. Anger is what they believe builds up the fuel for an abuser, and I can't lie, I'm angry. And from a lot of feedback I've had from therapists, people tend to hold on to silent/suppressed anger as a way to punish the abuser. If they let go of the anger they feel they are letting the abuser get away with their actions.

A light in this I see, is that 30-40 years ago when my mum was younger, the discussion of mental health and the important of child safety isn't as important as it is now, and there are great charities like NSPCC and a lot more safeguarding practices, so I hope as generations move on a lot more of this suppressed anger trickles down and it is dealt with so people can't build it up and allow themselves to continue the abuser cycle.

There are so many mixed emotions I feel about my mum's addiction. I get crippling anxiety feeling like I'm going to find her dead, next minute I am so angry at her for bringing this into our lives. Other times I can be like maybe it's what makes her happy so I just live with it. I think in any situation, a lot of people say to me "just cut her off", but it isn't always darkness. There are good times too. It isn't all doom and gloom.

Whilst this does sound like a constant sad tale, I have had happy times and there have been times I've been proud of my mum. What I'm trying to convey is that I never feel one emotion. Right now I'm sitting on the floor in my kitchen nearly crying then clenching my fists feeling like I could punch someone. You sometimes just have to ride the wave.

Only recently I found out that gym fanatic Joe Wicks had a heroin addict father, and a mother who had obsessive compulsive disorder (OCD). I have OCD and my mother is a heroin addict. He did an inspiring documentary on it, which I only watched the clips he spoke about his childhood admittedly, but I felt I wanted to reach him and tell him about my story. This is the first person I'd ever heard off who had heroin addict parents that you wouldn't have known based on the child and how they present themselves. He is the only exception from my previous comment about celebrities not getting back in touch, but he did reply and he has liked a few of my Instagram posts (@peneloperedtrust), which I am extremely grateful for. He's one of the good guys.

I have reached out to quite a few celebrities as the more I research, the more I've learnt how many names have suffered with addiction, or with addicted parents. For example, Cara Delevingne's mum has suffered from a heroin addiction. Sadly, at the time I reached out to Cara's representatives (which is a long shot anyway as she is a hot shot model in the US), a video emerged of her seemingly off her face on some type of substance, I wouldn't like to speculate which one/ones. It really hammered home the number of children that have addict parents do go on to substance abuse themselves. I truly believe this is down to insufficient support for their children and something I am hoping I can contribute to change.

There are also celebrities like Vicky Pattison who was known for being drunk and disorderly on a show called Geordie Shore, but has since come out and spoke about her experience of her father's alcoholism and how it affected her. Sadly I haven't had a response from her yet either, but she did like my Instagram photo.

Ever since I've been telling my story I've been thinking about how I can be as loud as possible. There is some awareness on children of alcoholics with it actually being spoken about in the Houses of Parliament recently with the likes of Calum Best, Vicky Pattison with association with National Association for Children of Alcoholics (NACAO). But it would be great to get the term changed to 'children of addicts'. We are all the victims of the same abuse, just a different substance.

I also reached out to (at the time) Duchess of Cambridge, as I know she is a big patron of children's charities and also addiction services. I received a weird response a few days before HM The Queen Elizabeth II died, in which she is now Princess of Wales, but it was just recommending some good charities to get in touch with, in which I have, and sadly they have said due to regional issues (me not living in their postcode area) they don't want to work with me. If only addiction could be harnessed by postcodes, but sadly it poisons life like coronavirus infection spreads.

I actually contacted my local Member of Parliament too, (not that I want to talk about politics in this as currently politics in this country divides everyone). He had agreed to meet me. We met at a local coffee shop, and he offered me tea. I do wonder if he claimed that back on expenses, but I thought it was extremely kind of him. We discussed my story, and whenever I do I see the people give me a look of pity. It isn't in any way to look down on me, but I can tell they do not think this should be the norm for a child. He called me a survivor, and that really struck me. What came out of that meeting was he understood there was a gap in awareness on children on addicts, and he had agreed to write a letter to another MP who could look at policies, so stay tuned.

There are so many different issues around the world affecting young people, and I think of all the causes I would love to support and feel passionate about, so I understand that one charity can't solve the world. And there is a lot I feel passionate about, domestic abuse, mental health but this is the story from a child of an addict, where society has failed me, and what we can do to become a community and feel less isolated.

As well as doing this book, I have been thinking of setting up a charity with the mission statement and I'm having talks with a multitude of charities including Women's Aid - whose slogan you may not know is 'until women and children are safe'. I've had quite a lot of discussions about my plans with people, including those who have worked with Women's Aid who didn't think they would cover stories like mine, but the response so far has been really positive. So, if you are a child or woman in need - please look at Women's Aid.

I am writing this because I want to help people, but also because I want to feel better. I hope by helping others it will make me feel like my experience was worth something.

I'm a lot better at selling myself in person, not that I feel this is a sales pitch, although it must have worked as you are reading this. I want to tell you my story and how it has shaped me. I have always felt I have a higher power, and no not like God. I feel my experience is supposed to help a future child like me. The future child who goes home from school and googles where to find their parents' heroin stash. I am still working on this, and I somehow hope this will help others.

There is still the quieter part around high functioning and heroin. It also does not help that Heroin is similar to Heroine (a woman hero). As Google puts it *'heroin* is sometimes confused with heroine'[4]. When I try and hashtag heroin or look up accounts linked to it, it always is people misspelling heroine or it is just the word heroine.

Alcohol addiction seems to have quite a good platform for discussion on Instagram, but that makes sense when you read this from alcoholchange.org.uk "Alcohol misuse is the biggest risk factor for death, ill-health and disability among 15 to 49-year-olds in the UK, and the fifth biggest risk factor across all ages"[5]

---

[4] heroin meaning - Google search

[5] https://alcoholchange.org.uk/alcohol-facts/fact-sheets/alcohol-statistics

Family Secrets & The Drug Trade

The reason my parents are the way they are is a construct of their own experiences, one that I don't want to carry onto my children, so if I do ever- publish this, it will be anonymous so my name will be blurred out so they'll never have to picture the things I have. I grieve for their respected childhoods, but my mum especially has allowed that to affect her children, and I am hoping to stop the generational trauma.

I have been reading a book where research was conducted on survivors of the holocaust and they found that trauma was genetically based down and led to babies being born with similar cortisol levels as their parents and grandparents. When I first heard this it scared me, like should I not have children? Am I dooming my children before they've even stepped foot on the world?

It's difficult sharing their secrets. I mean, they may never speak to me again if they knew. But when somebody offloads onto all your life, when does it become your secret too? I have already had a few threats around writing this, although it is all completely anonymous. Is trying to help other people worth possibly losing my family?

I keep feeling unnerved by the truth. It can seem such a hard balance between loyalty to your family, and your desire to help others.

I have found myself not posting certain things to protect family members, but it goes back to something I always ask, as well as the questions above; when does somebody else's truth become your own? If you are telling the truth can anybody be mad for telling your story?

I am quite often told "but it's made you stronger". I was a child. I didn't need to be stronger. I needed to feel safe. And whilst I have built some stronger walls then some due to my experience, I do not wish that experience on any child. I've learnt life really isn't about falling over, it's about how many times you get back up, and maybe that is the difference between my mother and me. I seem to be able to bounce back and not lay in the mud. Which isn't an easy thing to do, there are times I have wanted to lay in the mud, but I haven't.

Mental health was very different when my parents were young, so I do hope if they were born today things would be different for them. Even today we are looking at reducing the mental health stigma, ad I've tried to see how mental health was viewed in their youth and found this extract "Overall, the 1960s and 1970s were full of an anti-psychiatry attitude, blaming psychiatry for being repressive, coercive and more damaging than helpful to patients. The 1975 movie *One Flew Over the Cuckoo's Nest* in particular condensed this attitude against psychiatry."[6]

One big thing in mental health awareness was postnatal depression in which my mum suffered severely, with a lot of people thinking you were a failure to admit you were struggling. The same as being a sexual abuse victim, movements like #MeToo has really helped people come forward. There is still a lot of work to do with mental health but even seeing the difference from my parents growing up is such a vast improvement.

I love my family, I want to get that straight. The number of times I have gone back and edited a story to show someone in a better light or make it look like I'm not attacking them, then I realise I

---

[6]

https://www.ncbi.nlm.nih.gov/pmc/articles/PMC5007563/#:~:text=Overall%2C%20the%201960s%20and%20s1970s,condensed%20this%20attitude%20against%20psychiatry.

want to be honest. If I am not being completely honest I am doing exactly what I was brought up to do, make everything appear great. I'm going to show you behind the curtain, and I promise to draw it back all the way so you can see the cobwebs. Also in a way I promise not to over dramatise anything. You can still love your family although you are hurt by them.

I know, in some ways, I am lucky. I was never homeless, was in complete starvation or was deprived of education or hot water. This is not an invitation from me to you to hate my family or see me as a victim. This is a chance that if you have any of the same feelings as me, then I hope you don't feel so alone.

One thing that really grinds me down is when people have platforms and shy away from issues like this. I cannot tell you the countless people I have reached out to, including charities and celebrities who have told their stories via social media sites who won't even respond or acknowledge you, even if they could do good by just sharing or liking a post, I appreciate they can't see it all, but I know some of them have seen and not replied. And I hate to admit that I thought some of them would help for free. But sadly, I have learnt nothing in this life is done for free. Nobody will ever do something for you if they don't want something back.

Even subconsciously we do things for our loved ones, and why we don't want anything in that moment deep down we want love and respect back. The same as nurses want to be paid, or celebrities want money for a photo or supporting a campaign, the same as a nice therapist wouldn't help you if you weren't paying them. Even philanthropists, they are doing it because they get something out of it. Maybe not financially, but it will help them internally, maybe with their moral compass or for a sense of purpose.

Do I feel my parents owe me compensation? Yes I do. They did not offer me emotional safety and wellbeing so why not hope for financial help? Why do I want handouts? Why don't I crave that sense of 'I didn't get any help' or is it my inner child just wanting to be taken care of? Look how good my parents are? But I can't tell them or anyone because that is borderline emotional blackmail.

A question I get asked a lot: "Are you sure there is a demographic of people who are affected by these issues?"

Children's Commission Data reported the following *"478,000 children living with a parent with problem alcohol or drug use in 2019 to 2020, rate of 40 per 1,000."*[7]

Yes. I am not alone here - and this data proves that. But what makes it worse is that there isn't enough research and education. Nobody knows my mum is addicted too, so as reported by gov.uk *"60% of parents who are dependent on heroin are not receiving treatment."*[8] in that 60% or even more of heroin parents who don't tell anyone.

I wanted to talk not just about the exposure of drugs via my mum, but recently I've heard a really old dear friend of mine has been put in jail for 7 years for selling heroin.

So many thoughts through my head, some tears, because he's a good bloody person. I remember he carried my whole bag for me for a day, he was a sweetheart. His mum was so lovely too. His real dad never wanted anything to do with him, and when he was about 14 he tried to reach out to his dad and he got a terrible response. He was off with mental health issues for years and then re-emerged and I started hanging with him and smoking weed a bit. He was just looking to numb his pain I guess.

---

[7] https://www.childrenscommissioner.gov.uk/chldrn/

[8] https://www.gov.uk/government/publications/parents-with-alcohol-and-drug-problems-support-resources/parents-with-alcohol-and-drug-problems-guidance-for-adult-treatment-and-children-and-family-services

When I then met Lucas and had left that life behind me I hoped he would sort himself out. But no, he got dragged in deeper and deeper. I'd love to clip him round the ear, like what are you doing? Do you know what you are doing to people? And then I dread to think how he even got into that. How did you go from sitting on a park bench listening to Afro man getting the munchies ending up in your second prison stint in your mid 20s?

So many thoughts going through my head. 1 - I hope he hasn't sold it to my mum. 2 - I wonder if he is truly a horrible person now, is he violent? 3 - was he forced to get into this? Did he owe someone money and then this was his path? 4 - does he like this life? Does he look back and regret it or is he just chilling in jail?

He didn't deserve this life. We never think of drug dealers as the victims, but I truly believed it stemmed from his rejection from his father. I'm not justifying what he did, but I am seeing it as why couldn't his dad not have been a piece of shit. And why wasn't he supported better by the likes of the NHS?

And I've heard loads of people selling cocaine thinking it's really clever, like they're big shot business people. It's actually pathetic, or am I being harsh? It might seem cool now but you get caught and you have a completely different life in front of you. Growing up I only thought it was the big bad criminals that were selling the Class A's, but it can literally be your neighbour, somebody you went to school with or anybody you walk past. Even if they just sell it to their friends rather than running county lines.

I've tried party drugs and was borderline addicted to weed in my teens, so I understand why we do these things and what is attractive about them, not helped by my teen years being at the height Channel 4 TV series SKINS that made doing drugs look cool, if you do watch it, I can promise you it is not as fun as they make it look.

I've really been in my head about this, thinking where did it go wrong? Who is responsible for where he is today? Of course himself. And just because his dad rejected him does not mean he has a free pass to become a criminal and add to the ever-growing opioid addiction problem by supplying it.

The cycle of drug abuse is one of power and supply. Simple economics. Grow to fufil demand - Sell for a profit - Buy to get the high. It's a mutually beneficial relationship, of course depending on the drug we know the cartels in South America are very far removed to when you are snorting cocaine in the local nightclub, but it is a crucial part of the puzzle.

But in reality what is the part that would stop the cycle? Stop growing? Somebody else would. Drug dealers stop selling? Different drug dealers would step forward. BUT - we need to take more responsibility, yes us. If we didn't all buy some cocaine for the Reading festival making their supply massive then they wouldn't have anybody to sell too. Recreational drug use in the UK and the culture of doing drugs is rife. And whilst it might seem innocent to do at a random party because you are making sure you aren't becoming addicted you are pumping the drugs economy and adding to the supply and demand. There is no way we will ever stop drugs, but I do think we all need to take a bit more responsibility for the market of drugs and its place in our society.

And whilst we are reflecting on how our actions can be damaging, words also can too. I was reading a brilliant article about how we say 'they committed suicide' the same way somebody 'committed murder' and really we should challenge that to 'died by suicide'. This language is also open to criticism in addiction. I also want to talk about the fact I call my mother an 'addict'.

WeAreWithYou charity invites us to think about how we label addicts - this was taken from there Instagram:

Instead of saying…

Addict, junkie, alcoholic, or drug abuser

Try saying…

Person experiencing a drug or alcohol issue[9]

---

[9] https://www.instagram.com/p/CpmkZ_kqybe/

My Mother

Weirdly this one took me the longest to write. I haven't written this in chronological order so I've dipped in and out of the chapters. Maybe because she's caused me the most hurt, but this has been so difficult to write.

My mother, born March late 1960s to an Irish woman who had moved over in her early life, and her father who was not all present from her teenage years. I don't really know much about my mum's childhood. I know her grandparents we're quite well off, so was her dad. They even nearly moved to Sweden for his work. She did a lot of horse riding and had a financially comfortable life growing up.

My mum always had a good group of friends when she was younger and still has her old school friends on Facebook. I have seen photos of her as a teenager and she's really pretty and looks happy, but as we talk about in this, looks can be deceiving.

Since my mum has been in rehab (she went in summer 2022 for 4 weeks then came out and relapsed straight away), she has spoke about how her parents weren't there to drop her off at school as my nan would be sleeping all day, as she used a lot of sleeping pills called Valium. My mum has always described her childhood as horrific.

My mum is always the victim, even if she is the suspect/perpetrator also. I remember her being in rehab telling me about how horrible it was seeing her mother like that and how much it affected her and "woe is me". She did not have any self awareness at that moment that the exact excuse she has for shooting up every evening is the EXACT same position she put her two children in.

I know when she was 16 she decided to move to London. Gosh, when I was 16 I couldn't imagine doing that. Her parents dropped her off at the train station and didn't even wave her off. I'm pretty sure once she was settled in London she started dating a rich Arabian man who bought her a Rolex, in which she then got robbed of it. If that's even true.

She then got married to a random man who then later turned around and said he was gay. She's never really talked about their wedding or their relationship, but when she was with my dad they went and met him at Gay Pride so they still remained amicable.

Again, I am not sure on the timeline of where this happened, before or after marriage, but when I was about 16 my mum and I were watching a documentary about the serial killer couple the West's, and they spoke about how Fred West raped his victims and she just turned to me and opened up about actually how it had happened to her. She was walking home in London one night, and a man in a car pulled over and made her get in, I believe he may have had a knife/gun but don't quote me on that. I don't believe she ever told anyone and I think a lot of her drug abuse is to do with that. Even as I am writing this I am thinking, God she has had it so bad, I have never had that happen to me, who am I to judge her?

Whilst living in London, (I'm not sure if it was whilst she was married or not), she started doing heroin. I don't know much about this period of her life. But I know one of her close mates died from an overdose, which I've only heard second hand, I believe the reason my mum won't admit this to me is she doesn't see heroin as the problem, in my opinion. For her, she could never bad mouth or blame heroin for a death as she wouldn't be so stupid to do something reckless like that. So she moved back home to get clean, which she did, and she was working while going out with her friends, and seemed to be in a good place, which is then when she met my dad through mutual friends.

My mum and dad were both party animals, a lot of alcohol and party drugs (probably to make up for their childhoods). My dad had quite an aggressive streak when he got angry, and there's a photo from my uncle's 21st where my mum has a black eye from my dad when he was really drunk. My mum has told me a lot of stories about my dad, but I don't even know how much to believe anymore. My dad was and still is a flirt, he had slept with half of my mum's mates before they got together, which I think caused conflict. My dad then went to Australia and when they were back they settled down.

At this point, her mum had moved up north with a man following the split with her dad, and her dad had got with the evil stepmother from Cinderella - AKA Maggie. (I will talk about her in the next chapter).

A beautiful, traditional wedding happened. In a gorgeous church, which I've still got the wedding album form. My mum looked beautiful. My uncle (dad's brother) gave her away as her dad was missing from her life. I am very sentimental about the wedding. I have the album and even the newspaper clipping from the local paper in a frame. My mum and dad looked so happy.

My mum and dad were both hard working people, and still are. They then had my older sister and they worked opposite shifts so they didn't really see each other. They then decided to have me and that is when, from my interpretation of the events, seemed to spiral their life, finances and their lives.

My dad loved and in my opinion, still loves my mum, in a love of his life kind of way, I don't think he would go back to her as he is happy with my step mum, but he is still so twisted over her betrayal... I still feel to this day he knows her better than me. I've only known my mum on drugs and I always hear stories about her being really sociable, and it generally sounds like a completely different person. I do not know my mum sober, and that breaks my heart.

My mum and dad had a massive friendship group and was one of the first to have children, but before that they would go on holiday with their friends, go out with them, just generally always be out drinking and socialising. Some of my greatest friends are family friends whose parents when honeymooning with mine.

Prior to having me, they had moved out of her mum's dad place due to it being repossessed, and then moved into a council house for a short time while they worked on resaving for a house.

I believe my mum suffered from post natal depression, but she never looked for help. Back in the 90s it wasn't as voiced as it is now, as I discussed earlier. My dad was besotted with Lily and I, but I don't think he was ready to give up the party life, and my mum was. He would stay late at the pub while mum would deal with us, then she'd go off to work in the evening and he would take over. They ended up cohabiting and grew apart with the pressure of life.

My uncle's wife and my mum were really close, almost like sisters. In which she really steps up and helps my mum in the modern day. They used to go out drinking and I recently had a chat with my auntie and said to her "you honestly know my mum more than me, I do not know her sober". And it saddens me to say, but I only know the heroin addict mum.

In no way feeling sorry for myself, I am sure of certain elements of what happened, would have happened if I was born or not. My mum and dad didn't really have support from their families. They both didn't have a father figure, either through death or abandonment. Both of their mums were in difficult situations and had issues of their own, so they were not there to support them.

After they had me, they had saved enough for a deposit for a lovely 3-bedroom house in a cul-de-sac next to a park and a great primary school. The future was mapped out and things were looking good, finally, for the two good people who had a hard life and were finally making a future for themselves and their children.

This is where my mum wasn't happy with being happy. This is when mum threw a grenade into our lives and then had us kids and decided to cheat on my dad with the local junkie, then my step dad which I will cover in the next chapter. A few weeks prior to moving into this house, my mum turned around to my dad and confessed her lack of love for him.

I have gone over this many times with my therapist, but nobody can sit there and say to me that me being born probably was the catalyst of all of this. Sure, she may have ended up being an addict, but I think the pressure of a second child was just too much and sent her over the edge. I didn't choose to be born, so I know I am not to blame personally, but my existence is. Ultimately, my mum could have used contraception.

It is quite common for people to have self-sabotaging behaviours when they feel insecure or have fear, as taken from this website "Fear is a major factor in self-sabotaging behaviours. You may have a fear of failing or even a fear of being successful, which may seem unusual but happens when the path to success is stressful. It's not uncommon for people to fear what will happen when they finally achieve a goal, so they will engage in behaviours that make the achievement more difficult or unlikely. Insecurities may occur when a person doesn't feel confident or worthy enough to find happiness or achieve a goal. Insecurities keep people from pushing forward and reduce motivation.[10]

I mentioned earlier about my family friends (whom I still love and adore), but their mum and my mum were the best of friends in their younger adult lives. They were each other's chief bridesmaids, my mum was like adopted in her family also. But the

---

[10] https://draxe.com/health/self-sabotaging/

way my mum's mind works is that she was ridden with jealousy that her friend had a loving family, she started to just get annoyed at her friends luckiness as she would call it. Her father was rich so paid for them to have an extension when the kids came along, while my dad and mother were struggling while working double shifts. Instead of being happy for her friend, my mum pushed her away and wasn't the nicest.

The thing with my mum is she can be such a jealous and twisted soul. If I ever ring her with news about someone she loves to judge and pass comments because she's so unhappy and bitter. There is a saying that I think really relates to my mum "you'll never heal if you don't admit you're hurt".

My dad insists he went for custody, but my mum turned on the water works and said she'd have nothing to live for. My mum said she would let my dad have the house, so he lived there for a while, whilst my mum got a council flat for the three of us. As she didn't actually qualify for a council flat, due to her name being on a mortgage, she was asked to leave, so my dad moved out and we moved in. (According to my dad, he never lived there). My dad moved out into my nan's for a while, and then with my uncle, while he says he continued to pay for the mortgage on the other house.

We saw my dad a lot when we lived here. We would go to his on the weekends and stay on weekdays and he'd take us to school, he would even sometimes come over. I think my mum had assured him she'd broken it off with John and they actually took us on a holiday to Mallorca which was one of my favourite holidays ever (and one of the only ones I really had as a child).

My mum must have got off the drugs at this point, as she was incredible. She would go out drinking at night with the women who run the kids holiday club and Lily and I got treated so well as my mum was close with them. My mum even broke her toe on a drunken night out. Mum and dad took it in turns to look after us, and they insisted they were not getting back together. When we returned I think my mum relapsed and returned to her naughty teenage relationship. I will talk more about their relationship in his area later on.

This was all while my mum climbed the corporate ladder in her respected field. Credit where credit is due, her work ethic and her professionalism are second to none. And they do say a lot of high flyers, bankers/doctors etc. are high functioning addicts. But when you think of it you just think of a politician doing cocaine with prostitutes around don't you?

The house was sold, and I still get told different stories of how this went down (mum's side being they split it 50/50, dad's side being that it was more like she had 30/70 as she needed it for a new place for us).

My dad used his side of the money and got a flat, which is still one of my favourite places in the world. I have such good memories there or just running wild with my sister. His flat was on the top floor and we had a real Christmas tree once and he just threw the Christmas tree out of the window into the front garden and I remember laughing until my ribs hurt. By the time he threw it out all the pine needles had fallen onto his carpet. It was one of those moments I wish I could relive.

I am not sure what my mum did with the rest of her side of the money, I think you can be creative on what she did. She did save some as we did go on a holiday a while later.

After we left that house, we moved into another new build, a 2-bed house next to the sewers (I remember the shocking smell on certain days). I remember that house so vividly. Most of them are good memories to be honest, as it was mainly just my sister, mum and I so it was like the girls club just hanging out. I remember going in for the first time and being stood in the kitchen and my mum just being sad because John had been arrested again and she swore that was it between them. I have memories of him bathing us in her en-suite there so he must have stayed around a while longer, but this is where we were introduced to my step dad.

The hardest pill for me to swallow is how she got back into this. It is a big thing for me, is that you don't just do heroin, or find heroin addicts. She had to actively seek it out. It's not like you fall on a needle. For me, I just don't understand why my sister and I weren't enough. I know when addiction gets you it absorbs you and takes away feelings and emotions and your rational thinking, but why did she let herself get into that position?

I get the pressure of drinking alcohol. It is the only drug we have to explain why we are NOT using it. Access to alcohol and the social expectation to drink is in daily life. I am in no way saying any addiction is worse, but heroin is a lot harder to seek out than a bottle you can buy within any corner or major shop.

I do have good memories at this house, sometimes my dad would come over and stay with us here. We had a nice garden and I remember having a big living room to play with my Bratz. My sister and I shared a room and we would go to the local video shop and always rent out my favourite movie Kangaroo Jack, and give it back past the due date and pay a penalty. I never wondered why we didn't just buy it as I watched it so much.

My step dad at first was great. He was in his 30s and still lived with his mum so he had some disposable income. He had a luxury car and would always dress immaculate. I still remember being in a princess dress peeking around the bannister, being really nervous when we were introduced to us. After they were dating they booked a holiday to Florida. Yes, I know, I am very lucky to have gone to Mallorca and Florida (this is my last time before I met Lucas).

Everything seemed to go bad once we got back from that holiday. We moved to a village outside of where my step dad lived, so that meant leaving my hometown where all my family and friends lived, especially living with my dad was the hardest.

There were no more mid-week sleepovers due to distance and it really disconnected us.

With my dad being further away, my mum hid the drugs more. There is a photo I have of my mum in one of my albums of her chopping some food, and she is holding a bit of tissue on her arm. Why am I referencing this, you may ask. Because when I saw this photo I remembered my mum constantly walked around with her arm bleeding and her dabbing tissue paper on it. Our toilet bin would be full of little green bottles and blood-spattered tissue pieces. I always put it down to her eczema. I was so naive. It was obvious how obvious she was about it, just cooking will dabbing her needle mark.

Growing up, my mum stopped taking us out. She stopped being sociable and would always wear long sleeves as her marks got more noticeable. I thought it was more because of the bruises from my step dad. We never would go away, even for a weekend in the summer. I don't think I've ever really been swimming with her due to her never getting her arms out.

Eating with my mum is borderline embarrassing. If we ever do go out for food, she eats like a puppy who has been fed for the first time. She scoffs it down really quick then leaves over half of it. Everything is just such a chaotic rush. I invite her round for dinner sometimes and she has about 10 mouthfuls in 30 seconds then wants to leave.

A lot of drugs do damage inside and out. For example, drugs that you snort, after time your nose can show signs of the abuse with the middle section disappearing. Normally with addicts we expect them to be very slim. My uncle even said "your mum's a bit too chubby to be a heroin addict." She's size 12. She's normal for her age but she doesn't eat meals so she just eats sugary snacks and doesn't exercise. My mum was always tiny but she has recently started eating more.

I never understood why even on the hottest day my mum would wear long sleeves, or why she never took me swimming, and I never even saw her arms at home really. She would either have a tissue covering her arms or a long sleeve t-shirt on. I didn't know she was trying to hide track marks. What are track marks I hear you ask, they are discoloured areas, sometimes raised along the vein as a result of puncture wounds. They genuinely scab over, becoming bruised and can leave scarring.

I constantly feel like a bad daughter. There are so many children out there who don't have mum's through sickness or ill fate, and here I am choosing to have space from mine. It feels unjust. It feels selfish and unnecessary. I've always felt it was my duty to save my mum, and I've always had that parent role. I found a great quote that encapsulates this.

> "~~I feel like an imposter because I am fake at what I do~~
> I feel like an imposter because as a parentified child, I had to be an imposter
> I had to be a little mature adult"
>
> @jeanpsychologist[11]

After school I would pretend I didn't have a house key so I had to go to my friend's house to just have some food and get looked after. As I grew up I learnt to like the peace and quiet so once I hit secondary school I liked going home to an empty house.

I used to lie and say I was away for the weekend to my friends, even if it was just to Weymouth or something because I never did anything. Every weekend I would go down to the two couch potatoes, passed out whilst binge watching TV. They would never take me out, or bake with me, or pay me any attention.

---

[11] @jeanpsychologist Instagram*

When we first moved into the house in the village, I did dance one day after school, in which I reference later, but after that no hobbies I wanted to pursue were allowed. It was always "it's just a phase". On the flip side, my sister was allowed to learn the keyboard. I think they just saw more potential in her. When we were really little we did horse riding, and I always wanted to continue but Lily didn't like it. I pestered my mum for years and even now I'd still love to do horse riding. I think that is why I got into so much trouble at school. I had no outlet.

My mum is a good person, and I really believe that, but I also do not know her. I think the sober person is, or at least has the capability to be a brilliant mother. I see photos of her in her youth and think how wonderful she looks. She looks confident, funny and happy. I don't know that person. I know the self loathing, manipulative person who has openly admitted if I had parents evening but she hadn't had her fix we would miss parents evening as the drugs came first.

However, my step dad was abusive to my mum. I always hated him more for hitting my mum than hitting me. She was so scared of him and I just felt so sorry for her. But she went back to him every time, even when he was hurting us. I remember when he would just explode with his burning rage and force her into the car and they would go out for a 2-hour drive and Lily and I would just be worried if they'd ever come back. The phone would get cut off so we couldn't call our dad, or if we did, mum would quickly shut it down saying we were lying.

I know my mum was scared of him, God I was too, you'd be a fool not to be scared of that man. He loved portraying fear and intimidation, it was how he got his own way. The one thing I really struggle with is why my mum still sees him. I know it is to get her fix, but how can she do that after she knows he used to hit his two daughters? Is her heroin glasses stronger than her love for her kids? Whenever I speak to anybody's else's parents they would go to jail to stop anyone ever laying a finger on their kids, let alone have them over and watch movies with them and get high. And it's not even like she's sorry, as she's still doing it, so I can't even forgive her because she has no regrets.

I remember going to my mum's office once after school, and she only ever had a photo of my step dad up. Never of us children. It's the same in my dad's house, no photos of us. I don't know if that is a norm in parents that have separated to not have as many photos of their kids up?

I remember being young, my mum never really had any friends. All the school kids' parents would get on and arrange playdates. I didn't have any of that. My mum just kept herself to herself. She had work friends that she would occasionally see but she kept everyone at arms length. She loved just going home and getting high.

My mum tried with my sister and I, but her generational trauma really affected her. I am quite a cuddly person, and I remember used to cuddling her and she'd actually sit like a frozen statue and ask if I could get off. She used to always say to my sister and I that she shouldn't have children, which used to really bother me.

I talk a lot about being my mum's mother, as such, and how she was the naughty teenager who was sneaking around my back and she loved the thrill of it. But I was also her support system. I was the one she would confide in and tell me her worries. It is because she had no one else, which is really sad, but that is a consequence of her pushing everyone away. There is a term for this type of relationship called 'parentification'.

Parentification in essence is when the roles are reversed and the child becomes the parent. It can take different forms including bill paying, cooking, cleaning or emotional support. As mentioned, my mum didn't often cook as she didn't have an appetite. But she was on top of life admin. I remember bailiffs did come once and she always was paying off payday loans, but that isn't common with a lot of adults.

She would sometimes come into my room, and I remember one time she was showing me a website about a woman's rescue centre. She showed me how if my step dad would come into the room, they had set up this really good button to click and it takes you to a recipe for an apple pie as a quick escape. Although, my step dad knew something would have been up as I have never known my mum to bake anything in her life, so I think that would have made him more suspicious then if it was just on Google or something.

She talked about us going there for months. She had told me to start thinking about what few items I would take. I always knew it would be my favourite cuddly toy, who Lucas has welcomed too as I do still need my toy for comfort, and nothing else really mattered. I remember thinking how he would probably turn up and hurt us.

I was really excited that my mum finally admitted to me that my step dad was the volatile and scary pig I thought he was. He would always stick up for him, normally, or just make it about the fact I'm upset he's not my actual dad, rather than his behavioural red flags. I get it though, it is a lot easier to pretend the problem isn't there, because admitting it means you may have to take action.

Anyway, I ended up just being so proud of my mum, and thinking she actually cared about Lily and me. Finally she was picking herself and us, she was picking our safety and our future.

But it never happened. The reason my mum gave was that he has connections and he would have found us, which is quite plausible because he is a psychopath and knows the town we live in and I think even I could find out where it is.

The thing is, my mum did have other options. My nan would have had us, and offered too. But due to their fractured relationship my mum always refused. I also spoke to my dad about it, and he didn't think we should live with him. He will say to this day that he didn't know the extent of my step dad's physical and mental abuse, but I think that's a lie he tells himself, a bit like my mum.

My mum was actually a social worker for vulnerable people. She literally got paid for dealing with domestic abuse, drug and employment issues, social-economical issues, and she was often in touch with social services and rehousing abused children. So how she managed to do that day in and day out then came home and ignored the abuse she was receiving and then giving out baffles me. My mum knew all about domestic abuse and the great charities and support systems that we're out there. I'm in no way blaming my mum for not having the strength to leave my step dad, because it is so hard to leave an abuser, especially when you are scared. But I do question why her education and knowledge and access to services didn't allow her to act more than others who don't know what help is out there. Is ignorance bliss?

My mother confided most things in me, whilst she constantly lied about her addiction, she was very open about the horrors in life she has endorsed, such as her mother's valium addiction and her mother and father's absence within her life. I would be in the middle of my mum and dad's constant tale telling of who broke up the marriage and I just wanted to fix it all. I could never be mad at my mum because I felt sorry for her. If I was horrible to her then she would go and overdose. It was constantly walking on eggshells around her emotional instability.

There is another term for this which I wanted to talk to you about, I actually heard it on a 'Redhanded' podcast where a boy had killed his family, but they found his mother had been manipulating her son and treating him like a spouse or a close friend, rather than a child. A lot of it really resonated with my feelings with my mum. The word incest gets your back up straight away, but it is a recognised type of parental abuse. Choosingtherapy.com states "These parents turn to their children for comfort, love, advice, support, and in some cases, even romance. The child essentially becomes like a parent or spouse, which is usually more than they can handle."[12] Of course, my mum was not romantic with me, but I was more like her close friend or parent than her child. I was there to make sure she was eating and being responsible.

I always felt really grateful for my mum as she basically raised us on her own. I saw her more as a single full-time mum and I was in awe of how she would do an 8-hour day then come home and make sure she would do the washing etc. But she had a secret to make it work. As I've grown up, their childhood fantasies about her standing over the cooker have drifted away. She would rarely cook and she would never do anything with us, and by that I mean never would bake, or take us even food shopping. It has got to the point now where I never spent time with her doing things, it is just so unnatural to do anything like that with her. The only thing I have taken from it, is that I know when I'm a mother, I want to be in the kitchen with my kids all the time. I want to bake with them, even if it is just buying the premixed cakes and putting them in the ovens then doing silly decorations on, or doing their homework with them.

She did work really hard but I misinterpreted her dopiness for tiredness and always felt I owed her for working so hard for us. I am not blind to the fact that my mum did work hard. She did miss all of my sports day, and I had to go to after school clubs, not that was nothing to do with the drug taking. That was purely because she grafted all day everyday, possibly to fund the drugs, but I can not knock her for her work ethic.

If mum ever bought us anything like new school shoes (which was normally financed by my nan when we went to my dad's for the weekend), she would make us hide it and not tell my step dad as he didn't like her spending money on us. His control and spell on the whole family was like an infected spider's web. He was

---

[12] https://www.choosingtherapy.com/emotional-incest/

like a toxin in the air that felt us all with dread. He could switch too, one minute he could even have a sense of humour, the next it would be a war zone.

My step dad was from the army. I always thought that was why he was so regimented and strict. We had a photo up of him in his army gear as you walked in the house. The thing we didn't tell people was the reason he wasn't in the army anymore. The story I was told is that he and a good friend of his had managed to find some marijuana at one of their camps, (not sure if it was abroad or not), and they were caught and thrown into army jail where they were then booted for drugs. However, my uncle (the stoner), who knew my step dad prior to him and my mum becoming an item laughed his head off at the story and said to me it was a lot harder than marijuana, which now thinking about it, it probably was. Although the army is quite clear on their tolerance to recreational drugs as quoted from the army website: "any service person found to have used illegal substances will be disciplined appropriately, including discharge from service."

I went to two different secondary schools, and the second one my mum used to give me a lift sometimes if she was in the nearby office. We would always stop off at a house (I can remember the exact front door), and she would say she was just going in to get cheap tobacco. It was in one of the roughest areas where we lived and I would know what she was getting. I actually asked my mum recently if she still buys from there and she said no he died, she then went on a rant about how low life he was using crack, heroin and any substance and judging him because he smoked heroin instead of injecting it and how much worse that is because of your lungs. I don't know if she does this to make herself feel better but it is so weird how she puts herself on like a drug taking pedestal. I sometimes go past that house and I always wanted to call the police on it so badly, so at least I hope a nice family is living there.

My mum always compares and does compare my dad to her dad, and I really thought I'd lucked out with my mum. It's like, it doesn't matter if she's a drug addict, if she will spend £100 on me for Christmas then she is a great mum and better than those who don't have that money, even if they give their kids something better than materialistic items. My mum financially supplements my sister for her shortcomings as a mother, and she feels my father should do the same. So when my father doesn't give us money, like she does for my sister, she thinks my father is absent, but that shows her reflection on what a good parent should be, and I feel sorry for her. I knew she had no one and I have always felt responsible for her happiness. I still do.

My mum and step dad actually were expecting a baby when I was about 7 or 8, and she miscarried, I assume from drug use. I am so pleased for that baby that it wasn't born. And I know I sound like a monster, but it wouldn't have had a good upbringing. I was lucky in that my step dad wasn't my real dad and now I never have to see him again. I have none of his evil, wicked genes and I was able to escape to some normality in my other side of the family. Being ill-judged, I didn't think before they spoke to the child, I did say to my mum I am glad she miscarried at the time. That must have been horrible for her, and I couldn't imagine how that would have felt on top of just losing a baby, but I was clearly aware of the issues and how another child would not have helped our situation.

Like I say later on, my mum randomly booked a holiday when I was with Lucas for my sister and I to go to Egypt with her. But when we got back my mum was hospitalised. My mum and step dad weren't getting on at this point, and I was about 17 and basically lived with Lucas' family. My step dad was living at his mum's, which I assume is why my mum randomly decided to book this holiday. I will talk about the holiday and my mental health later, but upon returning from Egypt life got a bit crazy.

As well as a change in my mental health stability, Lucas' grandma was admitted to hospital and was slowly dying. We would go up most days to go and see her. I remember one day getting a call from my mum saying she wasn't very well and cancelled a hair appointment. The next thing I heard from her was that she was in an ambulance. She said about having really bad migraines a few days prior, but my mum and I have always suffered migraines.

When my mum was admitted, she was stable at first, and she had specialists from all over the country come to see her as they did not know what was wrong. At first my mum said it was just routine so I remember asking her for my driving lesson money (her and my dad financed some of them), and I remember my sister saying how ill timed of me it was, looking back it was mis judged from me, but my driving instructor was asking me for the money, and this is where my dad wasn't always very helpful. At this time I thought it was kidney stones as she has had them before and been in hospital for them. I do really regret that and I would hate my mum to think I don't care.

My mum then declined in health. My nan came down from up north and moved into my mum's house and would get the two buses up to see my mum everyday. She was really good. They knew it was a neurological disease, but they didn't know which one. They had told me they'd didn't even know if she'd survive as they didn't know what it was.

My mum then rapidly declined and was in an induced coma. I remember walking in to see her with Lucas's mum and just seeing her with all the tube's tied up to her and just sobbing into Lucas's mum's shoulder hysterically. I remember I kept calling the doctors every night asking for updates and they would never update me. Lucas's dad called them and complained also how they wouldn't tell me anything. This was partly NHS and their busy and hectic wards, but also my nan had a hand in this. I am sure it was mother's intuition that kicked in, but when my mum was on her deathbed, my nan would downplay her condition to my sister and I and I remember going there and my nan not wanting me to go and see my mum.

I think they must have realised that my mum is a heroin addict and diagnosed her with botulism disease. Botulisms are toxins that attack the nervous system and can be life threatening. My mum made a full recovery. She was bed bound for weeks so she had all bed sores and was on them milkshakes to fatten you up where she was so thin. She told me it was because of something she ate in Egypt, even to this day she won't admit it was the heroin. There are 3 types of botulism (as guided from the NHS website):

- food-borne botulism – when someone eats food containing the toxins because it hasn't been properly canned, preserved or cooked

- wound botulism – when a wound becomes infected with the bacteria, usually as a result of injecting illegal drugs like heroin contaminated with the bacteria into muscle rather than a vein

- infant botulism – when a baby swallows a resistant form of the bacteria, called a spore, in contaminated soil or food, such as honey (these spores are harmless to older children and adults because the body develops defences against them from about the age of 1)[13]

To this day my mum refuses to accept it was the heroin causing her to nearly die. And this really bothers me. Obviously it was the heroin. I ate what she ate in Egypt, and she certainly doesn't fit the criteria of an infant. And this is why I honestly don't think she will ever give up. I have never been addicted to anything, so I can only go from my own opinion, but if nearly dying isn't a catalyst to stop using then I don't know what is. And if you want to know what kind of person my step dad is, when my mum was in a coma he took her bank card and emptied it and spent all of her money on heroin, and yet she still sees him.

---

[13] https://www.nhs.uk/conditions/botulism/

All through this, my mum has been earning a generous salary and working full time 9-5. Since about 2019, she has been working from home more, as we all have if you are office based. This suits her as she doesn't worry about having to wear long sleeve t-shirts in the office when it is absolutely boiling.

I now see my mum every now and again and catch up on the phone. If I do ever go out with my mum, she is always clock watching and cannot wait to get home to get another dose. Even when I first moved into my house, she hardly helped, she came and saw it and left again. Even on my birthdays, not that we really did anything, but she's always in such a rush just to get back to her comfort zone in her drug area.

I hate to admit it, but I have picked up some traits from my mum. I can be really awkward like her, I can get easily irritated by people, and we both seem to be similar at work. My sister has also picked up some tendencies from her, especially her manipulative side.

I have always had such a pity for my mum. I have always felt she is dealt the worst cards in life, and she hasn't deserved that. And I do believe that, however, I resent her for always allowing herself to be the victim. She has also probably never sought help. Partly because there wasn't any, but in my mum's mind she has her 'medication'. She has used it for over half her life, for her that's like drinking water or going for a walk - it's a habit, a way of life.

My partner and I were having a really good conversation the other day on the back of something my counsellor had asked me. So I will ask it to you.

What *is* a good mother?

For me my mother provided me with shelter, clean clothes, lifts and adequate food. A lot better than other mothers, so I've always felt I was lucky.

But the mother I want to be, I see what I had as the bare minimum. I want my child to feel safe and loved. I don't want them to feel that their presence causes me stress and worry.

Lucas quite poetically put it 'a happy child is a good mother'. Of course, circumstances prevail including mental health and relationship issues but the core message is when you see a child in a happy environment who is cared for, it radiates through the child.

I decided to look up the meaning of Mother, and according to the Oxford Dictionary - "The female parent of a human being; a woman in relation to a child or children to whom she has given birth; (also, in extended use) a woman who undertakes the responsibilities of a parent towards a child, *esp*. a stepmother."

Mother or no mother, a bigger question I ask myself is should we feel sorry for addicts? Are they just as much victims as the people around them are? I try and tell myself my mum must like being an addict, that she's happy with the euphoria and peace she gets with it, but am I just kidding myself? I try and try to help her, but does she even want to help herself?

Sometimes I have the thought it may be better for my mum to overdose.

Wow, that is intense. I know this brings shock value, with the recent Book by Nickelodeon star Jennette Mccurdy "I'm Glad My Mom Died" (and for those over the age of 40, Nickelodeon is the channel for the home of Spongebob Squarepants), that statement has been getting attention. Not that I have actually read the book, it has brilliant reviews but a part of me doesn't want to admit I could feel like that too.

But it is important to admit these feelings, and I can assure you are not alone in this feeling. The more I am speaking to other children of addicts I have learnt this is a common trait and we continue to beat ourselves up over it, but we don't mean any harm to them, more we want to stop the pain and the worrying. I want my mum to get better, but I know all the stats on heroin users. I'm petrified of finding her one day. She had an ECG the other day for her heart and she said she didn't know what was wrong with her, and I made a comment do you not think it's your body slowly shutting down from the years of heroin? Blunt - I know, but sometimes you can't help it.

I hope that sometimes my mum likes being an addict, I hope she's not miserable and if she is then I don't want her to be in this pain. I wish I could take the pain away and stop wondering when she will get that bad batch.

My Mum's Parents

(The Irish One & The Unknown One)

I don't have the biggest story to write about my mum's parents. When she was older she lived up north and I would see her once or twice a year, and died in 2021 with emphysema, which is a lung condition which causes breathlessness. She would take about 5 minutes to walk up a little ramp and have constant heavy breathing, she died just before she would've needed a permanent supply of oxygen.

She wasn't the best mother to my mum, which I know my mum struggles with. She used to drink and smoke a lot, and wasn't always there for mum. They let her mum to London at 16, and they didn't even wave her off. I have referenced my mum's time in London so you'll know how that goes.

My mum's parents split up and her dad became a ghost father, and I mean this literally, I think I met him twice. Once was when he was really ill in the hospital and came to the realisation of what family he had missed out on (he recovered and this went all out the window). My sister, mum and I went to see a shrivelled old stranger in a hospital bed in a crowded ward where I wouldn't be able to tell you which one would be my grandad.

My mother's mantra she passed onto us was always "It doesn't matter if you are ok, as long as you look like it", which I think was passed down to her from her dysfunctional parents. It has led me to constantly think about how I am and I noticed myself and my mother doing the below behaviours:

- Being focussed on professional achievements
- Being preoccupied with your weight or appearance

- Wanting to do things very well or perfectly
- Finding it hard when you make a mistake
- Finding criticisms about your life, appearance etc. particularly hard to cope with

And actually links into the idea that you aren't a people pleaser, you are a parent pleaser. The people pleasing started in your childhood and you were trained to be one. You have been conditioned to fight for the approval of your parents and do what they expected of you to be loved. You've tried hard to break free from this toxic conditioning but it's not easy because it's deeply ingrained within your subconscious mind. It has become your default behaviour without you even realising it.

My nan had actually got together with a really lovely man, Dave, who I called Grandad (only after my Nan died, weirdly) and even though they live about 4 hours away we used to go up and see them at Christmas for 3 days and maybe spend a week with them. I always remember we used to meet at services near Birmingham. It was great going there as you didn't have to turn back around but going back you would have to go to the next junction and turn around, twice!

I don't know much about my nan's upbringing. I knew she grew up in Belfast. She was the youngest of many, many children - couldn't tell you how many. She would always say how her mum spent ALL day just peeling potatoes. Literally, there were so many of them and that was their main food supply. She went to a catholic school, I imagine it to be sort of similar to the likes you see on Derry Girls. Her father worked at H&W on the docks and got injured so they relocated to England. When she went to school in England, it was much different to the strict nuns teaching her. Her new friends thought it was so funny that she was brought up thinking holding hands could cause you to become pregnant.

She met my 'granddad' then in Newbury. I don't know much about their relationship or how they met. But my mother was born. She grew up in a modest house. I know my nan had a miscarriage with my mum's supposed-to-be baby sister. It was a still born I believe. I couldn't imagine how that felt for my mum expecting to have a baby sister then being ripped away from you, although my mum miscarried, she wasn't actually in labour like my nan was, so we hadn't gotten a room or anything ready and I already had a sibling. My mum has always struggled with being an only child.

I don't know much else about my nan during my mum's childhood, but after she and her husband split up she met a man in Warrington. He was extremely violent and would beat my nan black and blue. She ended up leaving him and met a man called Gregg who I now call Grandad (only since my nan has died). They met just before my sister was born and he had two children of his own. They stayed in Warrington and would come down and see us now and again and vice versa.

After they had split up when my mum had moved to London, my mother's father met Maggie. I've only heard about her from my mum and dad, but she seems horrible. She had a complex with my mum's dad being in her life. She had two children of her own who he was more of a father to. They sold my mum's childhood home to her and my dad at a massive price, no family discount, although you could say it was nice of him to sell it to them? Anyway, Maggie was horrible to my mum. She would tell mum's dad about how much of a horrible person mum would be and that he shouldn't contact her, so the weak man he was he cut off my mum.

My nan then moved up north and met a really abusive man who even put her in hospital. She left him and moved down and back up a few times, but then she met her future husband who became like a grandfather to my sister and me. Although since my nan's died, it's apparent how much my nan did the talking, as it is so awkward with her husband. Anyway, he made my nan so happy and had the patient of a saint. A truly remarkable man and their life was clear for all to see, and you wish they had met earlier. Although him and my nan had been together since she was in her mid 20s and all through her children's life, he never really had a relationship with my mum, probably due to her cold nature, but my nan had a great relationship with his children.

Although when you think about my mum's cold-hearted nature, I wonder what my mum would score on the Adverse Childhood Experiences (ACE). An ACE score is the total number of adverse childhood experiences reported by respondents. As the number of ACE increases, the risk for health problems increases in a strong and graded fashion.

Of course, there has been criticism for this, as just because you had an adverse childhood and you have a higher score you may not have as many issues as someone with a low score, so it is just a generalisation, not a certainty. As Dr Perry put it "Most basketball players are tall, but it doesn't mean every fall person will be good at basketball".

You can take these surveys online and they look at neglect, abuse & household dysfunction as outlined. According to KVG.org "It is estimated that 2 out of 3 youth will be exposed to childhood trauma before the age of 16."[14]

The three categories measured by ACE are Household dysfunction, such as having an incarcerated relative, divorce, domestic abuse, substance abuse and mental illness. Neglect is another, looking at physical, emotional and sexual experiences and finally abuse, physical or emotional.

---

[14] https://www.kvg.org

We don't know the extent of my mother and her mother's stories, but it is worth posing the question, where would they have scored within this? Anyway, back to my nan.

We would go to my nan's in the summer for a week once a year in the school holidays and there was such a difference between my relationship with my mother's mum and my father's mum. It was the little things, like she would get me really young child magazines even when I was mid teens, she just didn't really know me. It is lovely that she tried, and that she even did want to have us for a week every year, but we didn't have a deep bond.

I feel sorry for not praising her in glory, because I do love her. I do wish she was still here. But sometimes I can be too honest. When she did I cried, but I healed. Sometimes I think about how terribly she was treated and sat in a room dying all by herself being unable to talk and feeling angry and sad, but I can't sit here and say I really, really miss her. I didn't see her enough. I would love to hug her again, and get to know her more. It was only at her funeral when I found out more about her life and wished we had had conversations earlier.

My Father

Eldest of three to a woman who cheated on her husband, and whose husband was a drinker and part time father, eventually not being in their life. Died from a random heartache when my dad was 19ish. I will give my nan a section, because she is an iceberg so read that to understand my father more. He grew up being the man of the house. My nan had a thing for always selling their furniture so quiet often they just sat on the floor. They moved from Reading to Newbury in various council houses. No money, resulting in my nan stealing their food. At 16 he got a job on a building site to help pay toward his two younger brothers.

They used to hold these almighty BBQs at my nan's where they lived. My nan used to allow them to run wild and apparently they always had a house full. In fact, my step mum remembers going to one on invitation from my other uncle through a mutual friend and remembers seeing my mum and dad together, little did she knew she would marry my dad one day.

Now the next part cripples me to write, and I've had many internal battles thinking 'should I' or 'shouldn't I'. I truly believe knowing my family's history gives you a further understanding of how when broken people make people, they break them too. I feel terrible writing this, as this isn't my secret to tell. But my mum and Nan told me that my dad was abused by his uncle as a child. Fuck, that's heavy. My poor dad. Did my nan know and not do anything about it? What a bastard that guy is. His own uncle. Asshole. I wish my dad had reported his grossness. I really hope it doesn't haunt him. I wish I could take that experience away from him. He doesn't deserve that. I think his heavy drinking is a by-product of this.

They grew up on the benefit system, moving from council house to council house. The areas they grew up in are still known for being dodgy. My uncle moved there when we were older and my dad would tell me some horror stories. Like how he would get jumped just walking home from the youth club. When I think of anybody hurting my dad it cripples me. He has such a big heart you can see it when you look at him. He's got cute chubby cheeks like me too that you just want to squeeze, he is just so squeezable.

Now my dad was gutted when he learned I had been told. My dad doesn't speak about his feelings. He doesn't understand mental health. He has put your head down, move on, and get drunk every night to forget it. I just wish I could have gone back in time and protected him. That poor little boy.

My nan didn't really set any rules. I think they used to have like 40-50 people there, all hours, everyone welcome (which my mum would go to when her and dad were together, and weirdly my step mum went to one, and remembers thinking how beautiful my mum was - very odd. Dad doesn't remember her being there. My mum and dad met just after my grandad died (I think?) through mutual friends. My dad had a trip upcoming to Australia for 6 months, paid via his inheritance from his father's premature death (in which my nan actually used his cheque book and spend hundreds whilst he was away). They kept in contact all through his trip, with him even racking up some poor Aussies phone bills which allowed him free reign of their telephone, dad thinks it was way over £100... Especially back in gosh 1990ish.

When he got back they continued their romance. The first time he met my mum he said he was going to marry her. And he did. In a beautiful wedding in a gorgeous old church. I still have the printout from the local newspaper of it, and the photo album. They even went on a joint honeymoon with their best friends (who are my Godparents whose kids I am extremely close with to this day).

They had quite a heavy party lifestyle, being young, from broken families and a bit lost with no direction they both did the occasional party drugs (speed etc.) and drank A LOT. Which always comes with its own problems. Then they had my big sister. The light of their life, but according to my mum, my dad didn't really commit properly. He was always out drinking or at work, so the logical thing to fix their problems was to have another child?? Here I am. The little baby meant to be the glue of the family. Sorry mum and dad, but I didn't work.

They split before I can even remember. This is where it gets messed up. My mum cheated on my dad with the local junkie. I mean this guy was nice, but he's known for being a mess. He came from a great home and family, but he just was doomed to the life of the smack as they call it. My dad was shattered. Even to this day losing my mum still breaks his heart. You can see it in his eyes. She was the love of his life. Sadly John was my mum's. The irony of my mum being a social worker and going out with someone that was on all of their radars. Anyway we will come onto John too I guess as I am giving him considerable 'air time'. My dad moved out of the house and rented a little flat. He was gutted. He'd lost his wife and his daughters. And this is where the lines for me get blurred - Why didn't he take custody of us? But I will address that later.

My dad got into cocaine and gambling. My nan told me he owed someone a lot of money, but they overdosed or something so my dad didn't have to pay them back, although you have to take what my nan says with a pinch of salt. My dad does still gamble to this day, he loves horse racing even though I detest it and detest everything gambling stands for.

Before he met my step mum he had a one-bedroom flat and we just used to run rings round him, he would be drunk most of the weekend, but he did try his best, and my nan really did help. She would come and cook and clean so dad could watch movies and play with us. We used to see a lot of my dad's side of the family and he was thick as thieves with one of my uncles. He also had a massive social circle.

Where he's lived in the same town for most of his life whenever I used to go anywhere with him he'd always bump into at least one person he knew. He even knew someone at Lucas's football which is like 30 miles away but that just sums him up. I think where he used to go out drinking all the time he got to know everyone and anyone.

Whilst some of his friends weren't the best, he did have a few he'd known from school. One in particular was like another brother to him. He had a really solid family unit, and they took my dad in. They even took him on foreign holidays when they were younger. They are a little bit 'This Is England' so they aren't the most modern guys. They all have trade business' and live for playing pool in the pub on the weekend.

When my step mum came in she put a stop to all of his friends. They always invite him out, and he doesn't do anything without her.

Now I am older, my dad, step mum and I have a 'good as can be relationship'. His heart is massive and he is always the life of any party. He is extremely gullible and fully to laugh at and with, he is just a bit daft. He gets on really well with Lucas' family which means the world to me. My dad is really like that bit of normal I get to see now and again which is so important to me. He is a big drinker, and I think a lot of that is to do with his guilt and him suppressing his feelings.

But in the past year I've become a lot more honest with him and my step mum, and whilst it helps me to off load to them on what really went on in my childhood, (which I did think they knew more about, but they didn't know the extent of the abuse), I don't think it's the best for my dad's mental health. Every time he gets drunk he will ring me in floods of tears saying how guilty he feels.

He always says I've been such a rubbish father, and part of me thinks he does it so I say oh no you haven't dad and validate any relief of guilt. I think where he lives with my step mum too, she will always back up his actions even if they are wrong, so he is always backed up in a sense so sometimes he doesn't really do what he's truly done as he's constantly told he is the best dad in the world. He did get drunk the other night and called me and just was saying how guilty he feels and he's a horrible person. I was almost giving him a therapy session. It's not his fault, yes he may not have done as much as he could off, but I think it is a difficult situation to be in. Also, we have a good relationship now, so we have to move on. I don't want him to feel guilty, nor do I with my mum, I just want them to be happy and be there for Lily and me.

I've spoken about my step dad and his violence, but who is the man who I used to see every other weekend?

There are two sides of my dad. The broken vulnerable man who just wants to be loved and was grossly abused as a child. There is also my other dad, the drunk, won't take any responsibilities and can be extremely aggressive and is absent as a father.

I promised to be honest with you guys, and I've been silent around my dad, this has taken me the longest to write. I've chosen to withhold his impact on me because deep down I'm waiting for him to swoop in and save the day.

Fathers Day is always the time I notice it, you know the cards with BBQ champ or dad with the garden shed, I just look for the card with the drunk man on it, cause that's all I know of him.

I guess I am lucky I am in his life. But it is only when it suits him. Him and his wife have always gone on elaborate holidays and never invited us. I genuinely think when him and my step mum go on holiday and somebody was to ask them if they had children they would say no. I've never seen him on Christmas, my birthday, or his.

When we used to go over I used to love it when he would get really drunk because then he would end up being nasty and finally sticking up for us and himself to my step mum. I know this isn't nice to admit, but as a child I loved it. I have a memory of my step mum and sister picking us up from one of my dad's friends BBQs once when I was very young, and I was holding my dad up and I was laughing my head off thinking it was so funny, and because he wasn't ready to stop partying he started launching bottles of beer on the street so my step mum would go away.

My dad has never been violent to my sister or I, but he has got a reputation for it. My uncle has teeth missing where my dad got so drunk one night he knocked them out. There is a photo from my other uncle's 21st and my mum has got the biggest black eye, and it's from when my dad came home drunk and decided to boot her in the face. I remember seeing him rip my step mum's top at a wedding because she was supposedly flirting with someone else. At my mum and dad's wedding he had to wear makeup when he had got into a fight a few days before.

It is very easy to blame my mum for everything, but my dad has pretended he didn't know to avoid any responsibility.

What father accepts another man hitting his children and says nothing? What father hears his daughter ask him why someone has a needle in his arm and does nothing? What father doesn't pick up his children when they are begging him too? What father doesn't let his daughter live with him because his wife wouldn't like it?

He doesn't even really know me. I've never eaten fish and it's almost a personality trait of mine. (I can't really tell you where it originated from but I think it got heightened with the release of Finding Nemo, with the 'fish are friends' saying. I also think we shouldn't eat things from the sea, it just feels like it's not fair game. I can't really understand why I am so passionate about it, I just am.) Lucas and I occasionally go there and he offers us fish for tea, and it sounds so trivial but anybody who knows me would never ask me that and he just does it over and over again.

The way I see him is a 'fun uncle'. He is great when he's drunk, he can be a right laugh, to laugh at, or with. It's good to see him every now and again to have a laugh but you cannot rely on him for any emotional/financial support.

My dad always said he'd do anything for me, "he would die for me". And this is for my mum as well, is it easier to say you'd die for them than to live for them? You'd only have to die once, but you have to live everyday.

My Nan

When I think of people's life stories I don't always think the grandparents would be a big footprint in it. But in this case, my nan is central to how my dad, uncles, sister, mum and I all are today. Interestingly, I listened to the audiobook 'It Didn't Start With You' by Mark Wolynn, and it talks about how generational trauma can be passed down from grandparents and a lot of what they felt/dealt with we can unconsciously feel it too.

If you want to imagine my nan, think of The Catherine Tate show. I am sure she took inspiration from my nan. She is the racist, old fashioned, isolated, bitter but loving woman like on the TV. The first time my mum went over to my dad's for dinner my nan served her dinner in a dog bowl. That's the best way to describe her. How I describe my nan to people is if you told her the sky is blue, she would say it is green, but if you then agreed it was green, she would then say it is blue. She is an old fashioned true brexiteer.

My nan didn't have the easiest of starts to life, she was the youngest of like 8 or something, big in those days they seemed to pop them out in the high figures (similar to my other nan). I guess there was no contraception and abortion was illegal. There was quite a big age gap between her and her siblings so she wasn't as close with them as they all were with each other.

She was born in the war, and her mum walked out on them when my Nan was really young that haunts my Nan to this day. She never got counselling for this and this has affected all of her decisions. Her dad was her best friend, they were so close. He didn't go to war as he was caring for his children.

She told me a story about how she and her dad actually won tickets via the radio to go and stay in a hotel which had a view of Queen Elizabeth's II's coronation, and that is one of her most cherished memories. She remembers looking out of the hotel window and seeing the chariot/carriage or whatever you call it!

Sadly, he died quite suddenly when my nan was a child, which she is still HEARTBROKEN about. I go on about how she doesn't keep anything, but she still has some old dice of her father's which are her most treasured item. Following her father's death, she had no choice but to move up to Yorkshire to live with a woman who had abandoned her as a child. I can't even imagine how difficult that was for her, and she does not talk about it with any fondness.

She lived there in her teens then as soon as she was 16 she came back to her hometown. She then met my dad's father. He came from a nice family, and they liked my Nan. She moved into their family home and they wed then moved out with their three children. She did actually have an affair around when my dad was born, possibly due to housewife boredom. It does seem if you come from childhood trauma you do self sabotage your happiness. I know he was down the pub a lot, so I'm not sure if he was there for my nan, but when my uncle was born he really withdrew and then they had a third child, my other uncle then they split up.

They never had much money, and they lived in various council houses and he didn't support them financially. My nan even turned to stealing and was apparently in a local newspaper for being a prolific shoplifter. I do feel for those who steal food. When I worked in retail as one of my first jobs I worked for a nice company that sold 'nice to have' not essentials, and nothing used to infuriate me more when people would come in and steal a £40 bottle of champagne, or a luxury camera. I do feel for those who have to steal food, because they actually need it. Nobody needs a bottle of champagne or a camera to function like we need food. For me, I just feel sorry for those who have to steal food, and I would possibly feel differently if I owned my own business where I was losing money due to it, but my heart really goes out to those who cannot afford to put food on the table.

One of my dad's favourite memories however is once a week they would get a kebab, when my dad's youngest brothers were in bed and my nan and dad would do a sudoku together with a kebab. Really, that makes my heart melt. They always had second or third hand furniture and hand-me-downs, so that was one of their rare treats. My dad really took on the man of the house role when his father left. He even left school early to work full time to bring in money to help his mum.

I go on to talk about my nan's constant need to get rid of stuff, and my dad said it was no different when they were younger. She said they were constantly one day having a sofa, the next day she would have sold it. He said they basically just lived in an empty shell that they used as an indoor football court. My nan was quite laid back and not very strict, but she loved and still loves her boys.

My nan's husband then randomly died in his 40s of a heart attack when my dad was in his late teens. I don't think one of my uncles even went to his funeral as he was really only present for my dad for a small period. My other uncle was quite young when he died so he didn't really know him.

Though she never remarried, she did have a few partners before I was born. She even once made a pen pal with a prisoner in America and even went there and met him then she decided to come home. Nobody really talks about this so I'm not sure too much about that.

My nan has a bit of a complex with animals. I have heard stories about all of her pets going missing. I don't want to delve into that but make of that what you will. Apparently my uncle's cat 'drowned' in her bath whilst he was at university. She also allowed my uncle to grow cannabis in her loft (which he did get arrested and sentenced for).

As my uncles and father grew up and start having girlfriends, my nan really struggled with this. And actually my step mum said a saying to me once which made me cringe "a daughter is for life, a son is until he meets his wife", which I do not believe in at all and always try to encourage my partner to still see his mum which he always will. The boys had been my nan's whole world, and really her saving grace so she has a really toxic relationship with any woman that comes into their lives. I have mentioned her giving my mum food out of a dog bowl, but it didn't stop there. She would constantly argue with them, she even took one of my dad's girlfriends before my mum to get an abortion with my dad's baby.

My auntie had a still born and my nan blamed her that day for wearing heels. My nan even had a fight with my uncle's ex at my mum and dad's wedding day. To be fair to her, she did cheat on my uncle then had the audacity to turn up to her brother's wedding so she did deserve it a bit.

She is great with all of her grandchildren, and she has always been so good to me. She has known my mum and dad's complexities and tried to be there for us when she could. She would always treat us, let us have sleepovers, help us emotionally and financially, even though she doesn't have a lot.

At one time when we moved in with my step dad, we lived a bit further away from my nan/dad and my mum's work, so I would say I was ill and then I'd spend the day at my nan's. It was the best. We would go shopping and she'd spoil me in Argos, it was the only time I'd get treated really. I remember once when I was like 8, I had a Playboy stage and ordered playboy curtains, bedding and a lamp from the Argos catalogue. If only I knew what Playboy really was! She would buy me a new Nintendo DS game from the shop Game every time we'd go. I think I had about 15 games or something crazy.

My nan and I would always have really deep chats, even from a very young age. She is really into her horoscopes and has always told me how I am an Aries and whenever I had friends she would ask their star sign, she even checked to see if Lucas and I were compatible and we are. Although I don't need Chinese astrology to tell me that. It is quite interesting though as my mum and dad aren't compatible and they didn't work, and my sister and my star sign clash, and we do in real life. Not to get all spiritual on you.

My nan would be the one who would get me the winter coat and take me to Clarks and get me measured up for nice new shoes for September. I smile when I speak about her, because I know she has her flaws, but she has left an imprint on me deeper and stronger than a tattoo. I don't like to think about when she isn't here, but that day will come. That will hit me hard, because she is the biggest parental figure in my life. But, we have to take each day as it comes and be grateful for her now.

I have younger cousins and it's sad to see how different she is with them due to the age difference to how she was with us. She used to take us swimming and even booked a hotel for me and her once where we got crème brûlée room service! She's taken my sister on a mini break in the UK and we used to always get the bus or train to local cities. However, she couldn't even have my cousins over for a sleepover now. She struggles without her walker and can't go out without her scooter.

She was actually diagnosed with diabetes, but after a year of prodding her finger, and taking all the medication, she decided she was no longer diabetic, according to her. Even to the distaste of the doctor, one day she binned everything and announced 'she is diabetes free'. This is a great way of understanding how her mind works, and how stubborn she is.

Even though she has never had much, she has always loved getting quality items. She loves John Lewis, she could be sponsored by them. She shops at M&S everyday, getting her single jacket potato and small tin of beans as mentioned below and then her blue whole milk which is basically cream.

My nan has always treated us amazingly, and I am grateful for her for some of the tough times she's got me through, but she is hard work. They say hoarding is a form of mental health, but my nan has the opposite. Once my sister and I spent hours making her a birthday collage. We used all of our photos in my dad's loft that we didn't have any copies of. Two weeks later she said she posted it to her sister and they'd lost it. She doesn't even speak to her sisters.

She cannot even keep a can of soup for over a week. She constantly buys things then chucks them out. Her house looks like nobody lives there. She, like most people her generation, buy for the day, so she will go to M&S and buy a singular potato with a half can of beans or something of similar proportion. She also loves to boiling veg until it is mush. She is a little bit too old to go out now, but when I was younger we would quite often go out and have breakfast/lunch together when I was off school and she would always moan that things didn't just have salt and pepper on it.

At times she has been a friend, mum, dad and grandparent. A lot of people say being a grandparent allows you to correct the mistakes you may have made as a parent, and you have more time and less responsibility to be able to do fun things.

My nan is well within her 80s now and her health is declining. Seeing her fade away is petrifying. It feels like a part of me will die with her. Whilst I know she has her toxic traits, she is always there, day or not (although she falls asleep at 7pm), she is my rock. I've been feeling really numb about thinking what I will do without her, and I know you can't think like that. I know I need to go and see her more, and I try to call her everyday but it hurts seeing her getting thinner and smaller and more fraile everytime I walk in that door. Even though she takes 5 minutes to get up, she still wants to make me a cup of tea (if you could call it that, I would say more hot milk with sugar and a dip of a tea bag).

Thank you for everything, Nan.

My Mum's Lover & My Step Dad

The first of my mum's partners is John. John is the one my mum cheated on my dad with. John - A really nice guy. From what I remember, he was really good with Lily and me. He was in and out of jail. I can google his name and find an article of a drug bust he was involved in. When I was younger I thought if you went to jail 3 times you were in forever, like a strike system. I remember crying thinking he was going away forever. He was known as I've said before for being such a heroin head (is that a saying? It is now). I did question my dad on this. He always says he didn't swoop in and save us because he didn't know. But he knew John and his habits. When I called him out on it he said he called my mum and said to get John out of the house and he thought that had worked. Possibly a case of sticking his head in the sand? I can't pretend to know what I would have done in his position, being heartbroken by the love of your life, alone, still paying off a mortgage.

When I was about 5 I went up to my dad and asked 'Daddy, why has John got a needle in his arm?' I don't remember this, but my dad and family do. God what a harrowing sentence to come out of a young girl who should have never been subjected to this. That is a gut wrencher thinking about that. That's like some sad documentary shit where you start tearing up.

John did love us, I think. But he loved Heroin more, arguably like my mother. I remember when I was young my Gameboy went missing (I think that classifies me as a retro kid having a Gameboy). My mum generally thought John had sold it for drugs and told my dad. My dad being a hot headed drunk, who wanted an excuse to go off on John for stealing his life, when searching the town for him. Like a lion on a hunt. He had given up and went into his local pub, and to John's bad luck he walked it to meet the full rage of my dad. I believe he battered him in the car park. I knew all of this very young. Then my mum found the

Gameboy under my bed... Eek. The issue with this story is the fact my mum allowed someone in her daughter's life that she believed could be capable of stealing our stuff. In this case he hadn't and had just had an unfortunate beating. I don't really know how their relationship came to an end, but my mum knew she had to move on.

Even though I believe to this day her heart burns for John. She met my step dad. She told me she only married my step dad to ensure she didn't go back with John. I'm pretty sure she cheated on my step dad in the early days with John. When John learnt of the relationship he spray painted my mum's name and called her a slag on a building my mum worked for. Luckily they thought it was talking about someone who worked in the call centre but it was actually my mum's ex... Feel sorry for the woman who thought she'd been victimised though. Weirdly, I have had my name spray painted in an alleyway but this weirdo who liked me and I didn't like it and he called me a slag too. Like a mother, like a daughter? John returns shortly...

Introducing my step dad. His name is Neil. Not that there's anything wrong with that. He is the most traditional builder you could meet. He grew up in the roughest part of the town I now live. I wouldn't walk down there on my own... He has told me stories about being beat up badly by his father and once he said he was kidnapped overnight and tortured. Crazy. He was in the army, but got kicked out for substance abuse. He knew my uncle (we will come to him). He even told me about how he had crabs (the sexually transmitted disease) when he was a teenager from a dirty girl, when in reality he was the dirty one.

Neil lived in a town 40 mins from where I lived, so we moved over there which reduced the frequency of seeing my father. So my mum met Neil in a pub whilst grieving her finished relationship with John. They hit it off. Neil was clean at this point. He lived with his mum, drove a flash car and wore all the designer clothes. He smoked but I think that was it at this point. I remember first meeting him. Lily and I were in fancy dress at the top of the stairs too nervous to come down. He was nice at first. He actually has a kid of his own, which he doesn't see. He was a knob though. I'll talk about him a bit later. We moved to a nice village actually, I loved it there, Tory central but I loved it. I fitted in with the rich farmer lifestyle. Even though we left in a respectable 3 bed rented property in a cul-de-sac with a palm tree out the front weirdly.

This is a big regret of mine, but I remember being in a shop and calling him 'dad'. It didn't really stick, but looking back I can't believe I would do that to my dad. Sorry dad.

I remember Neil picking me up from the after-school dance club once (my mum always worked full time so we had to go after school clubs or be home alone) and I remember hearing him shouting. Reintroduction John. So my mum had run into John in a corner shop and he noticed the engagement ring on my mum's finger and got very distressed to the point he tried to rip it off her hand. My mum ran out to her car in a panic and called Neil. Now back to me downstairs hearing this shouting 'I'm going to fucking kill you...' and other aggressive terms. I'd never heard Neil like this and to be honest I was like holy cow what is going on. So I asked him and he told me John had attacked my mum.

The trouble with Neil really started when we moved to the next house, the one they actually got a mortgage on (dumb move) I am going to call it The House of Horrors. If those walls could talk, they would want to be knocked down and turned into an open garden free of drama.

Neil must have started on the drugs alongside my mum at this point. After they would work they would dose on the sofas like some lazy sloths all evening and only move to go out for a cigarette. We couldn't watch TV as Neil was. The only time we could watch it was before he came home.

They stopped going shopping regularly. Heroin addicts don't eat regularly. My mum just snacked on Twix. There was always

Cadbury Mini Rolls which I cannot stand now and them horrible Squares crisps (which are vile btw). My mum would always do a roast on a Sunday, I will give her that. Neil would drink Strongbow, he even had a Homer Simpson special glass he would drink it in. Send me thinking about it. He actually gave me loads of Strongbow once when I was young and I was steaming. I didn't know what was wrong with me but I was so dizzy so I went to bed, but now looking bad I was slaughtered, the stairs were spinning around me and I was clinging onto the wall for dear life. I don't think my mum knew he gave me a drink that time. He didn't do it regularly. He always invited me to have some. Although in France I'm pretty sure kids have a glass of wine at dinner with their parents so this isn't the most dysfunctional thing Neil did.

For a while Neil's kid was in the picture quite a bit. He was a year older than me and a year younger than Lily. The story around him was that Neil's ex-girlfriend said she was using the pill but wasn't and tricked him into having a kid. Neil was never really there for him, but his mum always tried to get him to be a good father. When we came along, we would often spend time with him. He had a few issues though, possibly abandonment issues from his father but he used me as a punching bag. Knuckle Punch sandwiches he called them. He was really into Yu-Gi-Oh! But I quite enjoyed that. My boyfriend actually used to like that so I have him to thank for showing me that, as Lucas wanted to watch the series with me. He got a burst appendix and got really ill, where he was constantly hospitalised and was like a big fat balloon because of all the steroids. My mum didn't really like him, nor did Neil, and him hitting me was the excuse they needed to cut him off. Poor kid. He went to school with one of my sister's friends and they knew him as the weird kid. I hope he is ok.

With Neil's child out of the picture and them living in their drug fuelled bubble, things got worse. My sister recalls a time (It has been erased from my mind), of her having to physically grab him off me when he was strangling me. She described me as being blue, she is still convinced he could have killed me. He had also threatened my sister that he would kill her if he ever came between my mum and him. He became an Ogre in our house ruling it with fear. There was a constant tense feel whenever he was there, everybody was on egg shells. There were no monsters under this child's bed, he was in the bed next door.

I remember being at my window once, and my mum had walked to the shops. I don't know what she had done but my step dad locked her out. I remember looking down on her and not being able to let her cry, and seeing her face as she was locked out in the cold. I'll never forget seeing that and feeling so hopeless.

We lived in a relatively nice house too, our neighbours weren't unemployed people, we had an Audi Convertible on the drive, everything looked great from across the street. Neil used to scream at my mum, I remember worrying that the neighbours would call the police, but they didn't. Maybe they should have. If he was really angry with her he'd drag her in the car and they'd go missing for hours. I'm sure he hit her a few times, I know he strangled her but not sure what else.

Neil knew all the druggies around the area. I liked it at the time as they would all say hello to me, like the big scary teenage gangsters. Now looking back that is concerning how 'in' with them he was. I had a best friend who lived in the local council estate. For the purposes of this we will call her Stephanie, her mum was a typical druggie. Their house smelt, they had disgusting white leather sofas that had discoloured and all the cheap fake leather had peeled off. They only had BBC so she only knew Tracey Beaker and loved coming to mine to watch Sky. Her mum was in the paper for GBH or something on her dad. I remember having a PJ day at school and my mum buying me new PJs from Asda for it and she was with us and she asked my mum if she could get her some too as she didn't have any. My mum didn't, which she probably should have, poor little girl. Later on she would be taken into care when she was a teenager when we didn't really speak which I think was the right decision.

I met her dad a few times. Neil told me not to tell him who he was because they'd had history. It turned out Stephanie's dad had been inappropriate with my step dad's ex when she was pregnant which wounded Neil up, so like any normal person he bit half of his ear off? I remember after him telling me that every time I would see her dad I could see the little bit of ear tissue that was missing. It sort of looked like he had cauliflower ears from rugby, but on the bottom of his earlobe. I couldn't imagine biting into someone's ear - that is just disgusting. They do say it's as easy to bite through your finger as a carrot but your body doesn't allow you to do it - I don't know if this is true and please do not try and do this and blame me. I hated keeping that secret from my best friend. I was petrified of it coming out and me and my best friend falling out. Luckily it didn't but we drifted apart anyway. I'm pleased to say she is nothing like her mum or dad, I don't think. I'm not too sure what she does, but I don't think she's on drugs, or at least the hardcore ones.

Bullies love you to be scared, but everybody was petrified of Neil. not that too many people come over to our house, but sometimes they would, but they wanted to know if he was at home or not. I think once he shouted at one of my friends really bad that I was then banned by her mum from speaking to her. I remember being at the park when I was younger, and my 'friends' at the time were actually taking the mick out of my outfit, but my step dad had come out to get me as we lived opposite the park and they all legged it thinking he would hit them if he found out they were upsetting me. His presence made the temperature drop. His disgusting smell and the way he conducted himself makes me shiver.

Neil's mum was a bit odd, but I think she knew Neil and my mum had their issues, and she really tried to include Lily and I in their family. We used to go round her big, rented cottage with a massive garden next to the stables and just play on the trampoline, or muck out the horses. She was a big Jehovah's Witness, so she made us go to meetings on a weeknight. I remember having to wear a dress that didn't show my shoulders or knees. I was never really into it but my sister got quite into it - she loves learning, so it was appealing to her. She even went to a conference in Cardiff for it. Luckily she didn't get to the door knocking stage. It was when she was told she wasn't allowed a boyfriend she was like oh sod that.

I remember once I found a needle and had told my mum, Neil took me for a drive. He just blamed my mum. He said how my mum had ruined his life and got him on it and she's all to blame. "I only tried it because I told her it was me or the heroin, and she picked the heroin so I wanted to see what all the fuss was about". I remember knowing something was up and always remember seeing green glass bottles in the bin (methadone). Once I went in to get some tablets in my mum's bedside drawer, and there were needles and a burnt spoon. When I asked her she blamed Neil, saying it was a one-time thing. That's when I crossed the T's and dotted the I's. I remember her pleading with me that she no longer does it, in which I stupidly believed her.

I remember looking at TalkToFrank about heroin. The only thing I knew about heroin was that my uncle's best friend died of it. Imagine being a young girl reading - Risk of overdose and death is high. Possession can get you up to 7 years in prison, an unlimited fine or both. Driving while high is dangerous and illegal[15]. There is a lot of information there, but generally it's scary. My mum would drive me high as a kite everyday. I was so terrified about telling anybody in case my mum lost her job or went to jail and it would all be my fault. And even as I'm looking on this webpage there is a help section. Worried about; a friend, a child, or pressure to take drugs. There really is nothing about parents. I am actually looking online to buy some drug tests to possibly make my mum do well if she consents, and there is only about buying them for your children.

---

[15] https://www.talktofrank.com/drug/heroin

Did you know TalkToFrank is government funded, and the latest update I can see on there is from 2013? I have tried everything in my power to try and find out who runs it to get in contact with them as their website has so much credibility and influence, but it really isn't being used to its potential. It also doesn't have all the other risks of heroin like botulism etc. Even on Instagram, as I am hashtagging drugs it comes up 'learn more' and it takes you back to that exact website.

He used to make Lily (my sister) and I do the weirdest dares, which I still think are kind of normal but everyone tells me they're not - I'd love somebody to tell me if they think this is normal? My step dad never sexually assaulted us, you'd think that was to be expected, a child not being sexually exploited, but the number of horrific stories there are out there, and what I have read and seen is still haunting on how common it is. I want to make that clear.

But he would offer me money to run around the garden naked in the dark. He only did it once or twice, and I still can find excuses for it, it wasn't until I told somebody that they looked at me like HE DID WHAT? I did it, because I'm the funny one, remember? I did anything for a laugh, that was the only thing I was reliable for. He also gave my sister £10 to lick the front of his motorbike where all the fly guts were. He used to poke us. Like in the chest. A grown man poking a child would leave bruises. I will go on to talk about this later in the failings of my school.

Neil loved moto GP and even now to this day the sound of motorbikes goes through me like a dagger to the back. We could never watch TV if he was there or it would just be the sound of motorbikes revving around for hours on end. I actually bought a Mini Moto once for one of my birthdays, I only ever went on it once so I'm pretty sure it got sold for drugs.

Neil is still a present issue. He is still married to my mum, and she still sees him (and lies about it). Albeit it they don't live together. Actually, she lies so much, when Lucas and I went for a curry with his parents near my mum's, I wanted to invite her. I didn't want her to be sitting at home on her own. So I rang her and she coughed, like in Mean Girls, and said "I can't. I'm not feeling very well". We were then driving near her house in which I said 'that's my mum's car', to which I was going to beep, but as I sped up next to her we realised she was in the passenger seat, and my step dad was driving. I then rang her again, and gave her the benefit of the doubt, and said how are you feeling, in which she continued to lie saying how she was in bed and couldn't move, to which I called her out and she hung up on me. She generally is my pathetic naughty teenager.

I talked about my holiday to Egypt with Lily and my mother, but something more scary happened when we were back, which I haven't actually ever really thought about.

My Sister

My beautiful older sister. I have a lot of guilt over my older sister, because I don't know if I've been the best sister. She is beautiful. And I was always jealous of her, well her looks and brains, not her personality. I was always compared to her, rightly or wrongly. I do go into this in my section on secondary school. We couldn't be more different though. The saddest thing about Lily is that she won't talk about our experiences. She thinks she has conquered the past, that it no longer affects her but it does.

She has decided to live a life of the 'show life'. I don't blame her, but I also don't think it's entirely healthy. She has just met a really lovely boy which is promising, but before she was dating a lot and drinking a lot too. She does the occasional party drugs due to pressure from her friends, in my opinion.

Even to get into university, where my mum didn't really put us into any extra curricular, Lily needed so many hours of hospital voluntary work as well as a musical or sport skill to get into dentistry school. When she was doing her A-Levels she would do 6 hours a week at our local hospital with end-of-life patients and then she'd go to taekwondo after. She deserves the success she has.

I think part of the reason she was so determined to go to university and do medicine was to get far away from our home situation. She had a long-term boyfriend whose family was like hers, sort of like how Lucas' is mine. If she came home from university she'd go there.

However, Lily never took on the parental responsibility of mum like I did. She knew what mum was, and she wasn't going to change that (albeit since I've had a break from my mum the last few months she's really picked up on the parental role of looking after mum, and I think she's realised how much I did for all these years). Mum never used her as an emotional soundproof like she did with me. Like all my family have.

My sister is an air head, but I think that protects her too. Whenever you speak to her it'll be all about how she is and how her day is, and if she's in a good place you won't hear from her. She doesn't have the self awareness to think about others, but again, I think this is her brain dealing with her trauma. I've spoken about trauma a few times now, but what is trauma?

> *Trauma - noun - A physical injury or wound, or a powerful psychological shock that has damaging effects* [16]

I saw this recently and found this really insightful. Trauma is extremely unique and somebody could go through the same "experience" but have different traumas. Take my sister and I for example. We both lived in the same house, with the same parents. But I chose to go to T Total and I had a mental break. I continue to blame myself and feel I am responsible for my mother's sobriety. Whereas she feels so crippled she feels it is unhealthy to talk about it and internalises it.

They say trauma is the way our body responds, and our childhood trauma is biological as well as emotional.

In her course of medicine it attracts a lot of private school applicants. Partly due to some of the private schools having fast tracking systems into certain universities and affiliations. My sister was actually offered a scholarship at a top private school in secondary school, which she turned down, which till this day I will never understand why - I wish I had the opportunity but that isn't what we are here to talk about. I guess like her time at

---

[16] https://www.oxfordreference.com/display/10.1093/acref/9780199534067.001.0001/acref-9780199534067-e-8554;jsessionid=D913C5C0E55C3737598CBEDF864D5719

university she knew she would be the poorest child out of the lot, although from stories I've heard they can be rife with drug abuse in their life. According to an article in The Independent *"Girls from top private schools three times more likely to suffer from drug or alcohol addictions in later life than their less affluent peers"* [17]

Living around and with private school girls gave Lily an inadequate capital feeling. The first years in halls weren't so bad, but the other 4 years she was living with 3 millionaires and another girl who was in a similar financial situation to Lily. They would buy Chanel bags like Lily would buy a Primark bag. She had a part time job as well as doing her full time studying and hospital work. I think this is why she didn't want to go to private school when she was offered the scholarship, as she wouldn't be able to keep up with the other girls and their luxuries.

However, Lily has picked up some traits from my mum and step dad. Rightly or wrongly. I am sure I've picked up some too. My sister has a f*** you feeling towards my parents. And she played them the best she could. She would get my dad to pay her minimum credit card payments every month, whilst my mum gave her £400, yes, £400 a month, each month for 5 years. My mum did it out of guilt I believe, and felt this was making up for her using.

My sister also got a bursary for her amazing grades. I was working full time and Lucas and I had been together about 4 years and been on one holiday together, she was a university student, and one year she went on 5 holidays. To this day it still winds me up as I felt she used mum for every penny she could have. Maybe I feel wound up, because I was always honest and

---

[17] https://www.independent.co.uk/news/education/education-news/private-school-pupils-drug-alcohol-addictions-more-likely-new-research-money-fake-id-a7766951.html

helpful, but I've never really been helped. And I don't even know if I would want it, but shouldn't things with kids be fair?

Lily has a bad temper, like my dad and a bit like my step dad. If you ever meet my sister, which none of you will, do not cross her. She looks like a gorgeous model, but then she turns into Jackie Chan. She used to absolutely batter me in fights. I should have known better than not to start them but I always thought one day I might win. That day never came! Once she came at me swinging a hair dryer and hit me over the head. She's spat in my face before, and through my favourite teddy out the window which I still have not forgotten nor forgiven.

But then I did wind her up, this isn't woe is me. Lily put up with a lot of crap. Whilst she always had so much attention from boys until late secondary school she found it hard to make friends and would often end up being bullied (out of jealousy I think). Not that I considered that at the time. But I was just so jealous of her. It wasn't even like she was the pretty and sporty one and I was the creative one, because she was better than me at art too. Society always makes it seem there's a fair balance in the world but there's not. It's not "you have this or that". I still don't really have any talents. Not like Lily. But I want my honesty and my story to change someone else's, or even just to relate.

All the boys used to say to me 'why can't you look like your sister', in which I'd respond I know! I am biased as I am her sister but she was generally the IT girl at school. She always dressed lovely and presented herself lovely. Although we still call her stinky Pete as she hated showering. Although Lucas did point out recently that is probably because we never grew up with showers, so for us we just had our couple of baths a week, which isn't that strange, but as we grew into our late teens, we were the only ones not to have a shower. I remember we would stay at my dad's and we would be excited just to have a shower when we'd go every other weekend. I'd spend like an hour there with the radio playing. I'd be in there so long I'd put the plug in, let the bath fill up and then have a bath after my shower.

Even now if we go out for dinner I'll end up paying even though she probably earns more than me, although she does have to pay rent in London.

Lily is a good person. She has very different values to me which makes us hard to connect. As I delve into later I am very particular about ethics, conduct etc. And sadly Lily and I clash nearly every time we see each other. I love her like my best friend, but sometimes I wonder if we are both too broken to fix each other. Maybe I am not a good enough sister. I will carry guilt for making my sister feel bad for being amazing for the rest of my life.

In fact, in wanting to write this she was unsupportive. She wanted to read it to know. But a memoir isn't supposed to be edited. How can I hope to display my experience as true as it is if I blur the lines? But it's like Instagram and social media, in real life you can't just airbrush that spot out. Or make your friend a little slimmer. I've actually left a lot about my sister out, because I want to keep this story's impact on me. She currently has an overpriced life coach in London who tells her basically to get loads of money and rule the world to happiness and bury all the crap before. Nearly everyday she tells me how my counsellor is crap because I focus too much on the past.

They say when you have childhood trauma, a part of the 'post traumatic stress disorder' that you have an urge to relive trauma. This is the way of replaying memories or visiting old people/places either because they feel safe or trying to figure a way to overcome it. And this is why I find it really hard when my sister doesn't even want to talk about my past with me. It feels as if until I sit down and talk about it with her I feel like I could have made it all up, like I need that validation from her that we did go through it and she had the same experience with me.

When I was really bad with my OCD, and I was told I couldn't carry on with Sixth Form, a big achievement for me was going to meet Lucas or his mum for a coffee or something, or walking

Brambles (Lucas' family dog). She would text me "that's it go eat your coffee and cake and don't work". I forgave her for that as I thought she just didn't understand mental health, but actually she's just not learnt how to love properly. It is a shame because we could've been each others' rocks, someone to run too in the darkest of times, but actually we seem to drag each other down more than pick each other up.

In fact, we went out recently and she used the term about her friend's "OCD" as her friend likes the flat tidy. I contemplated whether to say anything or not, because I am not the OCD police, but for her knowing everything I went through to use that as a personality trait or preference hurt me. I know it was ignorance, but it did upset me.

My Uncles

My dad has three brothers, and they are really well representative of the 'class' system, if you still believe or read into that. You have my dad, the oldest, a self employer decorator who earns a decent salary, loves horse racing and golf. He would represent the 'middle' class. Then you have my dad's other brother, the middle child, who is the biggest stoner you will ever meet but has the best intentions and the sweetest heart. Worked in the same job for 30+ years, works so hard grafting all day and can't wait to come home to a Stella Artois and a spliff. He would be known as 'working' class. Then you have my dad's youngest brother, a bit of an arrogant twat, but that's his way of coping with the cards he was dealt. He is a partner in a firm, lives in some fancy cottage in the countryside with his American wife and my two cousins who I adore. He would complete the three-class system on the 'upper' class.

I want to start with the middle uncle. One of the nicest guys you could meet. Wears ridiculous graphic T-Shirts Tesco sells. You know the one with the terrible puns on? He was the middle child. His father never warmed to him. There were rumours he wasn't the son of I guess technically my 'grandad' although he died years before my mum and dad even met so I guess he's just my dad's dad. He was always the trouble kid, there normally is one in the family. I was it until I turned 18, now I'm like the model child, if I do say so myself.

He started smoking weed when he was about 13 and he's never come off it. My nan let him grow weed in his loft, which got raided, and my other uncle (the posh one who was back from Oxford University at the time) was there and he actually originally got arrested, which I hear didn't go down well. Imagine coming to your mum's for a weekend and getting arrested?! My other uncle did eventually get charged when they had worked out this misunderstanding. My uncle served time, I think about 2 years, when my sister was a baby. I was told they used to use my sister to sneak him in drugs. They used to put it in her baby grow and pass her over. Only weed, nothing more hardcore, not excusing it but at least she wasn't a crack mule. He served time with my dad's abuser, their uncle, nice family reunion?

He is the same age as my mum, and they got on so well. As mentioned before, he even gave my mum away. He has always been supportive of my mum, including having her around for Christmas a few years ago with my sister. He is very aware of her lack of family, and still treats her like a sister. My mum is a very closed book though and doesn't let him in. My uncle really does have an open-door policy. I know I could go round anytime, any day, any how and he would always offer me a cup of tea and make sure I'm ok.

He's all about the little things. I used to love going round to see my cousin's while I was younger. He lived in a really rough council estate, which still to this day I wouldn't go too unsupervised. He had a little flat and he constantly hot boxed it so we were all probably high as hell when we went round too. His house had no boundaries. As long as you let him watch Formula 1 on TV whilst he had a smoke, you could do what you want.

Make potions in the bath? Turn the bedroom into the biggest den? Get everything out of his cupboards? Not an issue for him. He is really good with kids, and we all loved him - probably because we had no boundaries. We could stay up all night, and he had put a shed in his garden just for us kids to play in. It was completely different to my own dad. When my dad was single he was the same, and would do anything for us, but when he was married, we had to fit around his life, when we went round we couldn't be kids as such, but my uncle just let us do what we wanted. He would always give us £2 to go down to the local shop and back then that would get you a can of fizzy drink and a fair few bags of sweets, so we were just constantly on a sugar rush.

Introducing my other uncle. Never really been present in our lives. There is quite a big age gap between my brother and my other uncle and this uncle. There's only a year between my dad and his second brother, but then there was about a 4 to 5-year gap and I think the younger brother wasn't as close as the other two. He also is very different. He was very quiet. He grew up on the council estate and had the same upbringing as my brothers, but he didn't go out with mates from round the area as much, and was much more of a mummy's boy. Due to the other brothers being a bit older, he got a lot more one on one time with my nan and was raised quite independently. I think they were also a bit more financially stable compared to when she had the first two.

He knew growing up he wanted better in life, he wanted to change his narrative and be successful. When he was 16, he had work experience in a practice, and they offered him a job if he completed university. Back then, it was very rare for anyone with a less privileged upbringing to go to university, but he put his head down and he made it work. He went to Oxford University, and loved life with all the Toffs. He is rugby obsessed. I think as he was coming out of university, my older sister was born. He is quite quiet and generally only socialises with people with money. He has his trophy American blonde wife, and they have their own unique relationship. They've been together for years. They're very sociable with 'there kind' and massive drinkers.

I still remember when they got married, they only had my sister as a bridesmaid. I still remember dropping her at the hairdressing sessions and the dress fittings and being sat in the car with my dad fuming I wasn't there too.

I think now she has kids, she can reflect and realise just having one of the kids wasn't really fair, but a lot of people like having just one cute child to be a bridesmaid. I remember at the wedding, we were all sat upstairs on the children's table except my sister, she got to sit on the top table. She also got a beautiful present for being a bridesmaid, and my sister didn't even care for it. There's a beautiful picture of Lily in her dress with my dad, it's such a lovely photo and memory for her to have.

Funnily enough, my auntie did ask me recently if I was still mad at her for not having me as a bridesmaid and if I would just have one of her kids involved in my wedding, in which I replied (I don't lie), something along the lines of I don't sit there and cry about it but it did hurt and that both of her kids will be involved in our wedding.

I've never really been close with this uncle. I remember when my sister got her GCSE grades (she was in the newspaper for getting 11 A*s and As, absolute genius), he turned to me and said "it won't be like that when you get yours will it". My uncle has always thought really little of me and so much of my sister. Possibly because she went to university like my uncle.

I wanted to follow his footsteps in his career and to be like him, as I always sort of wanted his approval. I always felt like he was my inspiration, my role model. I felt like he would accept me if I had the same big job as him. Even now in my role whenever I see him I feel like I want him to hear how well I'm doing just to almost prove myself. But I don't need to prove anything to him. I am the one who contacts them, if I didn't offer myself to them and offer to babysit I would never hear from them, and that is the cold hard truth.

So that is the crux of my family. Those are the main players I grew up around and helped shape me as a child.

The Misunderstood Child

A lot of my childhood is a blur. We lived in so many houses and towns I never had a solid base, and the place we settled in the longest was my biggest nightmare. I was always told I was a really cute child, I had big chubby cheeks which I still do and was always the comic of the family. I was quite cheeky and loved playing.

What comes to mind with my childhood is 'it's not how you feel, it's how you look'. My mum was very clever at making sure not to bring attention to us in any negative connotation. She even worked with vulnerable families and would come home and tell me how lucky I am compared to some of the families she goes to that abuse their children, pets, and home. So many of us are taught as kids and adults to hide dysfunctional or abusive households by keeping up appearances. I think my mum thought if she denied and justified her actions she would believe it as well as getting us to believe.

I was lucky enough to have a Gameboy and then a Nintendo DS. My nan would always buy me the latest Mario game. I used to have a habit when I would lose on Mario I would bite the top of my Nintendo screen. One day I bit it so hard the screen pixelated, of course I didn't tell the store what actually happened, and because they had never seen anything like that they gave me a new one and I made a clear note to self: DO NOT BITE IF YOU LOSE.

My nan was a massive part of my childhood and she really has got the love and respect from all of us grandchildren. Whilst she spoils us in terms of giving us sweets and fizzy drinks when our parents said no, or always making us hot milk with added sugar which was our absolute favourite.

Throughout the craziness of our parents, nan would take us to paint our own pottery or for ice cream and just do normal stuff with us. I remember going to my dad's every other weekend and snippets of my step dad and my mum's old boyfriend but Lucas always tells me stories and I don't remember as much as he seems to.

I don't remember a lot of my teenage years to be honest, I have to think quite hard. I remember just being a nightmare to be honest and only caring about having friends and the most followers on social media, which I did get quite good at, which is the complete opposite of how I am now. I have a private account that I don't let anyone follow. I don't understand if someone isn't my friend why would they want to see my most personal posts?

I actually moved secondary schools for a range of issues. One being I started declining in school, and my sister was going out with a boy from another school and my sister and I really wanted to go there, it was also close to my mum's work. I got excluded for 3 days at my other school for pulling a girls hair, which is very out of character for me (bit of context she did message my sister saying she was going to bury me the night before), so my mum thought maybe it would be good for me to be with a different bunch of people. God how she was wrong.

This school was known for better results than my previous one. It did have a lasting legacy of having a 'hammer attack' in the tennis courts due to a racist incident. Based on the geographical area of my new school, it had a much bigger and varied catchment area, rather than being in a small part of my town, this was in the village and attracted local farmers, villagers, mid-town and small parts of town like myself. They ran school buses, although my mum was never organised enough to get me a bus pass. I would either get a lift in with her or get on the local public bus with petty cash out of her purse. There were a few instances where she didn't have any money, so after school I had to walk in the dark miles (it once took me 2 hours), or I would have to go to a friend and wait for her to finish work or sneak on the school bus.

Whilst I don't remember a lot of my home life at this time, I randomly get a rush of memories when my senses are reminded of previous trauma. What do I mean by this? So we all know the 5 senses, sight, see, hear, taste and smell. Trauma wounds can be reignited by a word, a smell, a sound and even a type of food. There are a few things that can bring back harrowing trauma for me, one being mini rolls and the other is the song "This Love" by Maroon 5. It is a great song, but whenever I hear this I feel physically crippled. It is my step dad and mum's song. You know, every couple has 'their' song. I remember hearing it from their room when they were planning their wedding.

It can almost make you feel you have teleported back to that exact place, that exact room. In fact, it is said that complex trauma can impact a child's development of their sensory system in daily life. So much of us is shaped from our experiences, and we aren't taught how we unlearn these reactions so we can move forward.

I told the school once about Neil hitting me. I plucked up the courage to tell my mentor. I showed them my bruised chest. I couldn't risk telling them about the drugs, but surely this might finally get rid of the beast in the house. Finally, I had spoken up and ended the status quo, or so I thought. Surely once the school knows you're being hit, there's no way back?

It takes so much courage for a child or anyone in that fact to come forward and talk about their home situation and abuse. One of the main reasons I was not believed is due to my mother's appearance and full-time job. They called my mum, in which she said I was lying. That I must have either made the bruises myself or done them on something innocent at home. My step dad was clever. He wasn't stupid enough to leave marks on my face. He had an image to sustain. They believed my mum and dismissed me as an attention seeking teen. How can you be in a place of welfare for children when you do not safeguard them? I'm still so mad at my mum for loving someone who hit their child. I was always more sad he hit her but now I have let go of feeling like her parents and I am so mad she didn't protect me.

The same person I told about this was my at the time mentor, which is a word I do not carry with great respect giving she was more of a glorified child sitter. I remember she once said to me 'you act like you've been raised by wolves'. A bit of context, she was referring to this as I had an ear stretcher big enough to fit a whiteboard pen in.

I think about how if Lucas went home and told his parents that their parents would probably kick off big time, but when I told my mum she didn't really care. She didn't engage with the school, nor did I want her too. I just think if I was a mother and some teacher had said that about my child I would be making a formal complaint.

I would love to sue the piece of crap. I'm so angry at you, School. You failed me so hard. The ignorant teachers, because they thought I made up stories about being abused, sent me on a drug course with a drug counsellor who used to lecture me how my cannabis use could turn into a heroin addiction. Do you know how bad I wanted to scream at her "I'M NOT GOING TO DO THAT BECAUSE I LIVE WITH TWO HEROIN ADDICTS". But I knew I couldn't because I would be taken into care. And I knew care could be worse. You see the news, and people being abused in care homes. I knew my situation could have been better than in a care home, and I was with my sister.

Far too many kids are written off or told they have behavioural issues rather than having facilities to support them. There is a good quote 'humans take a while to change, systems take even longer'.

I felt I must be the only child with a heroin addict parent because I couldn't find anything. The stories on heroin only seem to concentrate on the homeless and unemployed who get mixed up in petty crime, but my mum didn't fit in that bracket so I had no support or guidance. Society almost acts as if you can't be a high functioning heroin addict.

Please. Do. Better.

Please can everybody all agree we ALL have a duty for safeguarding.

Please can everybody agree to stop writing troubled kids off without looking into what happened to them – not what's wrong with them.

I still have my struggles, but I now know I am not alone in what I faced. Since openly talking about my experience throughout my childhood (within the safety of Instagram without my family knowing) I have had so many messages including somebody saying they can sleep better knowing they are not alone in what they have been through. Any child of an addicted parent needs to be seen and heard.

When writing this, I have researched a lot about what a memoir should be, and I don't just want to sit here and tell you all about me. So, within this section I researched into children with behavioural issues like myself, and what support we can give them. A brilliant example of this is the work Dr Bruce Perry has done.

Dr Bruce Perry talked about how one teacher reminded a boy of his abusive father, so he lashed out. He was told off and labelled as a problem child, when actually, it's because that teacher triggered a subconscious link to that child and the fight or flight kicked it. That child isn't broken, he just needs support.

I do wonder if psychology should be taught as is biology so we know how our brains work as well as our blood and nervous systems.

Consequences Beyond Belief

I spiralled in school. My sister was an A* student and I was not dumb but not clever. My sister was even in our local newspaper for our GCSE grades. She was always gifted and talented, whatever that means. And normally one child is artistic, while the other one is academic, nope she generally was better than me at both.

I was in middle set everything, and sat under the radar. But I cried out for attention. How I received that attention was through misbehaving. It got to the point where I had my own seat in isolation and I was really close with the people in the isolation unit. I basically ran that place and they loved me.

I remember we would never have lunch stuff, so my mum would sometimes give me lunch money and I would meet all my friends at the local shop, have a cigarette that my mum would have just given me and any spare change she had (about £2, if that), then I would go in get a can of Dr Pepper (95p) and some Tangy Toms (25p) and a creme egg, which this shop did all year round which was awesome. And that is what I'd eat for the whole day. Normally in the first period, if that isn't a warning sign I don't know what is. I ended up scrounging lunch off my friends or stealing a cheese and bean panini. I actually got one, they just asked for it back they didn't care about the circumstances of why I needed to steal food.

I was the class clown, and I did some really funny things looking back. I guess you could compare me to a female Bart Simpson, and I was strangled by the father figure in my house too, two peas in a pod. But I was a little terror. But that girl was just crying for help, and nobody answered her call. I had an ear stretcher once and was told I was raised by wolves. Not far off. In my counselling session I have been asked to give compassion to that little girl. It was only recently I realised how bad my childhood was. It was not ok what I put up with, and still do put up with.

I had a mantra I lived by in my teenage years. I enjoyed watching Two and a Half Men, like a lot of before, and thought Charlie

Sheen was a fascinating character. He had a saying that at the time really resonated with me and something I took on until I met Lucas. "The best way to not get your heartbroken, is to pretend you don't have one".

I chose myself. I chose fun, or at least what a teenager thinks is fun. Staying out till 2am, drinking, smoking and trying to have as many friends from different schools as possible. Some of the groups of friends I had were good people, some weren't. That's when I knew that I needed to change. A number of them had difficult upbringings and some had gotten into drug dealing and crime. Once I wanted to buy some cannabis with a friend and I knew someone who had just gotten out of jail, and a drug dealer wouldn't sell to me because they thought I was setting them up. That's when I knew this shouldn't be my legacy, and I am better than this.

I remember being younger and my sister and I would be sat in the back of our car begging my mum and step dad not to smoke in there as we HATED the smell of it. We thought it was scum of the earth. So why years later, did I pick it up in my teens and no longer had the same hatred for it?

I was listening to my favourite book (audio) What Happened To You, and they are talking about how our body produces small amounts of opiates naturally. Whilst opiates are found in the opium poppy plant the natural opiate is a bind receptor in our brain.

I have never self harmed, I won't even get a tattoo I am scared of anything sharp and permanent, however a lot of people do. Why? Our brains react in different ways, for example someone with a normal stress response becomes over active and this is a way the disassociate. They can tolerate the cut but for someone with a sensitively overly reactive response it will feel "good" and the opiate burst can feel like a drug hit. Dr Bruce Perry talks about this is great detail in Chapter 6 and other ways of those with abuse such as chronic chaos then your neurobiology becomes sensitised, and we find ways to soothe.

I always wondered why my mum would do "toxic" things to herself, like cutting, injecting herself, but when someone has that neurobiology they are just looking to disassociate.

I was also walking one day with my friend to the shops and these two girls stopped us and asked if we knew were to buy weed. We must have given off vibes that we smoked it, we were only 15 tops. We responded yes and made a few calls to a few of our friends who asked if it was for us in which when I said no they hesitated. They had a bad smell, and to be fair they were right. One person picked up and agreed, so we walked with these two random girls until we approached the dealer. He handed over the goods, until one of the girls pulled out her key and threatened the dealer and he walked off. I felt so bad, the girls then just ran off and I never saw them again. Of course, I didn't know that was their intention or I wouldn't have arranged the meeting.

I was a bit chubby. When I was younger I had a lot of 'puppy fat'. My sister was horrible to me about my weight, always calling me fat. My step dad and mum would laugh, and just say I'd lose it. I remember saying to my sister I was a size 8-10 and she said don't lie, when I actually was, so now I will never think that size is good enough, and I constantly drive for a size 6 or I feel like a massive whale. Whilst continually just to fuel me on Cadbury Mini Rolls. It is a little strange, how someone who wasn't given a lot of cooked meals and was generally always hungry, could be slightly overweight. It wasn't like I looked malnourished. To the outside, I was a well fed, clean clothed child with two full time working parents in a normal home. But it was not normal. And it took me 24 years to realise that.

Mental Health & My Diagnosis

I want to talk to you about my mental health. I do truly think my mental health is a large consequence of my childhood, but I am not qualified enough to say I wouldn't have had any of these issues if such events had not occurred.

I am also diagnosed with obsessive compulsive disorder and generalised anxiety disorder. I don't like to think of them as defining me, more as they are a side of my personality that can come out.

Obsessive Compulsive Disorder is something we hear a lot, as I discuss, but Mind Charity's website really puts it poetically:

"Obsessive-compulsive disorder (OCD) has two main parts: obsessions and compulsions." … "It's not about being tidy, it's about having no control over your negative thoughts. It's about being afraid not doing things a certain way will cause harm." … "You might find that sometimes your obsessions and compulsions are manageable, and at other times they may make your day-to-day life really difficult. They may be more severe when you are stressed about other things, like life changes, health, money, work or relationships." [18]

I do have OCD, but I don't need a pencil to be 30 degrees towards me. If I had a pound for every time somebody told me they were OCD in the workplace or at home because they like a book in a certain position, I would probably be on holiday right now. That is not to say that some peoples' OCD doesn't conspire into how things are organised, however just liking something a certain way is just being human. So please - if you take anything away from my story, be more mindful when using throw away comments such as 'I'm OCD'.

---

[18] https://www.mind.org.uk/information-support/types-of-mental-health-problems/obsessive-compulsive-disorder-ocd/about-ocd/

My family always says, looking back, I did show symptoms from an early age. For example, I would need to know what activity we're doing but also what we were doing next. I was always uncomfortable in new settings and tried to control every aspect of my life. I also struggled badly in school, but they put that down to misbehaviour as I spoke about. I remember I would have to start walking on my left foot and end on my right, or go back and do it again, and always wake up at midnight and if we got past 1 o'clock I knew we wouldn't be broken into and we made it through the night safely.

Whenever I would stay at a friend's house I would have a panic attack and be sick and my mum would have to pick me up. Even though I was properly safer at the house I was staying at, it just gave me awful panic attacks.

But it really started on a holiday with my mother and sister. I was in sixth form, my sister was just about to start university and I was settled with Lucas. My mum booked a random holiday to Egypt for My Sister and I, didn't ask us, just booked it. I know some people will be reading this thinking, you're complaining at an all expenses paid trip to Egypt? Don't you realise how lucky you are? I hadn't been on holiday with my mum for about 14 years. I couldn't even go on a day trip with her without feeling claustrophobic, embarrassed and trapped. This just summed her up. I was never allowed to decide anything for myself. I had NO CONTROL. Anyway, I was upset about going on holiday without Lucas, and nervous at spending a whole week with my mum but excitement grew.

I remember the first sense that something wasn't right was, at the time, I was studying textiles, and wanted to become an interior or fashion designer (I know - predictable right?), so I got Alexander McQueen's biography to read on the aeroplane. I also studied Psychology at sixth form, so I was quite interested in mental health etc. However, when I was reading about Alexander's struggles something resonated with me, and I felt scared reading it, almost because I could relate. At the time I put it down to the nerves of the holiday and I have never, ever picked up that book again. On the holiday, I had a breakdown. I wanted to come home, I wanted to feel safe. Egypt isn't the safest, and whilst it was lovely, my mother and sister were quite nervous so we didn't leave the hotel complex. We were surrounded by a lot of women in full hijabs who were quite vocal about the fact we were just in a skimpy bikini. My sister is a very pretty girl. Always has been, and I remember a creepy guy taking photos of her. I was sick and hardly ate. I got into the routine of only eating at 2pm when they'd do chips by the poolside. Every day I just counted the days till we were home. I'd think to myself, Ok so after dinner tonight I'll only have two more dinners here.

Getting home and seeing Lucas was thrilling. I never wanted to leave him again. He'd been on a lads holiday to Bulgaria so it wasn't separation anxiety. I think it was the fact I was made to be without him without actually wanting too. I remember him having a football match the next day. His mum, dad, sister and I would always go. We loved it. I still try to go and watch him. I just remember feeling a bit numb. I thought maybe I was ill, but the numb feeling didn't go away. I'd lay there at night and just feel empty. I knew it was nothing to do with Lucas. I just know it felt like a part of me had just gone numb.

The only constant throughout my downfall was Lucas. Him supporting me. When I would wake up and just cry. When I would get sent home from sixth form for just bursting into tears. His family have been great and are like my own family, but at the time they were probably concerned I was going to be a 'high school dropout'. I knew there was something wrong with me, and it was so scary. I did call Samaritans a few times, but at that moment I couldn't see a way out. I didn't think I could ever feel normal or myself again. And in some ways that is right. I am not the same person I was before my breakdown, maybe that's partly down to ageing and maturing, but I do look at the world differently.

At this point I thought I was just broken. I went to the doctors who just said I was depressed. I kept going back, begging for some help. I remember in one instance I sat down and told a doctor if you do not help me I want to kill myself. They sent me home, with no help. I changed doctors, and was prescribed some medication which did help and referred to CAMHS (Child and Adolescent Mental Health Services). I remember just wanting to sleep, and although now I still love a nap, it was therapy sleep. I would cry myself tired and I would always go to sleep by picturing Lucas and I on holiday.

6 months later I got an appointment, to which I had an elderly woman say to me, maybe you just have an issue with your boyfriend or just being a teenager, and you'll get over it. I knew it was nothing to do with Lucas, he was the only thing stopping me from killing myself. And I mean that. I didn't want him finding me and him having to go through life with that trauma. He did not deserve that.

At this point, I had missed so much of Sixth Form that they said I couldn't come back. That broke me. I was unemployed, uneducated, my dreams of university were gone and I could barely leave the house. I applied for different jobs, in office settings/shops but I never lasted in them. This caused a lot of angst between my family. I was so scared I was never going to be able to work and just be sat at home hating life forever. Then I read back through my A-Level Psychology. Still with the diagnosis of depression I knew this wasn't right. I wasn't depressed. Luckily I had the resources and knowledge to look further. I realised my intrusive thoughts and my rituals represented OCD. I remember going back to the doctors with my findings and they said 'oh yes you definitely have OCD'.

The pressure from my family and Lucas' family was also intense. Nobody knows if I was just going to be a bum and never work. There was a lot of ignorance around my mental health at that time. Lucas' family didn't want me just sitting in their home (quite rightly), all day and not working, eating their food and using their electricity. I can understand it even more now I have my own house, especially as I am writing this in 2022 and the cost of living crisis. I am a stickler for turning every plug off. I won't even have Alexa on!

I still had the feeling though that I didn't just want to do any job. I remember once I got a temporary job working in a clothing warehouse, and the people were so different. Some of them were on parole, they all were sleeping together, I remember just going to the bathroom and crying uncontrollably. I lasted about 3 days there. I didn't even get paid for the work I did! It sounds quite judgemental, I know, but I was brought up to be like that, I guess? At least they're working, and a job is a job, but I knew I wanted a good career, which I have managed to get.

The number of jobs I have is incredible, and now I can look back and laugh. I've worked for a bridal designer making wedding dresses, I have been an apprentice marketing assistant (although that lasted one day), I've worked in many shops. I just couldn't handle them, and I was so scared I would never be able to work and just function.

I then got another part time job and something just clicked, I was able to do it. I was still on my medication, which had finally agreed with me. After that I got another job and got the taste for a thriving career. It's really weird though, I am funny about having friends with people I work with, and once I leave a job I cut them all off. It's a very toxic trait of mine, I know. It's like once I've taken a step forward I couldn't dare look back. I look at photos of myself from old jobs and think I couldn't actually work there now, how did I do it? I generally get a sick overwhelming feeling if I see anyone from previous jobs.

A few jobs later with a few promotions, I got a new job in the pandemic, and my OCD hit bad. Really bad. It can just come from nowhere. It was a massive pay rise, with a similar company and similar flexible home working arrangements. I just remember after meeting my new manager on the first day and getting home and crying. I even messaged my old manager asking for my job back. I did start this job when our mortgage was going through, so I think it was just a lot for me to cope with. I couldn't sleep, which normally when I'm stressed I sleep too much, so this was new. I'd never understood how people can't sleep. I just laid there and thought about how much of a mistake I've made and how I can't do it. I didn't eat for a solid five days, which also isn't like me. I made myself physically sick and just went to everyone crying hysterically how I couldn't do it and I needed to quit.

I think it was a combination of anxiety, imposter syndrome and the change, which is common in all of us. What adds to this is the OCD layer. It adds the new compulsion to it, I have to act. With the amazing encouragement of my partner and some deep-down grit I stuck at it and I love it now, and I do really good, and I've had some tougher times whilst at the job and I've been ok, so I'm more resilient than I think. I have often shied away from looking at other jobs because I am so scared this will happen again, and I'm scared I won't come out of the other side. I was offered a job recently and declined it, and I have actually just accepted a new job and all the intrusive thoughts and anxiety are starting to rush through, hopefully with the tools and all the money I've spent on books I should be able to work through my emotions better.

With OCD you get intrusive thoughts. Not just the rituals, but the obsessive, thought provoking and scary thoughts. And the more you try to stop them the more they grow and fester. For a while I didn't know why they were. And it's taken me about 7 years to learn you are not your thoughts.

But my OCD is a gift in its own right too. Like I talked about earlier, what other 24-year-old woman, with no degree, is a project manager in the construction world? Whilst my OCD creates an anxiety that has stopped me from working, I also think it has given me such high standards for myself. A component of that is running away from my past too, and also my mum does and did have a great work ethic. The aim isn't to be rich but to be comfortable. My passion is going to Liverpool with Lucas, to be able to go to as many games in a session would be our dream come true. Not hospitality or anything like that, although that's the only ticket you can get. Anyway, when I got my first full time job at a department store I knew I wanted to work my way up.

I did online courses/CAD training and landed myself at a job where my mum worked. This is where I met one of the most inspiring men (bar Lucas) I will ever meet. He became a father figure and a mentor and if this ever gets realised it will be down to his belief in me. Whilst he was stern, he showed me what an impact I could have on this world. He has taken me to football games I could never imagine going too, gave Lucas and I experiences that don't happen to people like us. He gave me the confidence to realise I am more than going to work and coming home. I will and want to make a difference. One day at a time. I don't want to be famous or rich. I want to help others and allow Lucas and I to live and be free. To have financial stability and finally feel I can cut the cord between my family and me.

My mentor left the organisation and I knew I needed to push myself out of my comfort zone. Nothing good happens when you don't put yourself out there. I applied for a project manager position in another organisation in a similar workplace with a salary increase, all while our mortgage was going through. Sadly, my anxiety and crippling OCD took over. I started in the height of Coronavirus, for those who may not be reading in the height of the 2020s, this is where we all locked down into our homes. So nobody was going into the office, and starting a job remotely is very odd, I have to admit. I didn't sleep all week, didn't eat and cried and made myself vomit due to fear I couldn't do the job. I was so scared about quitting and losing the house and ruining all my happiness. There is also a nagging feeling that I will go back to when I was in sixth form too, where I didn't even leave the house. Even though I'm not that young girl anymore, who didn't know what was wrong with me, I am constantly crippled by the fact it could happen again.

Lucas and his family was amazing in this. Since I started the Dolly Parton 9-5 working full time, they've been amazing with my mental health. They always make me believe I can achieve what I want too. I will always remember Lucas' uncle is a very successful man, and he said to me 'don't apply for jobs, do loads of courses then people will want you'. And of course, I have had to apply for jobs, but the mantra really stuck with me, and I just watched YouTube videos on construction, and did a free online architecture course online, I paid for an interior design diploma... You get my drift.

And with my 'big great job', and my average but high salary for my age range, it comes with risk. As they say, the higher you climb, the further you fall. I could see how scared everybody around me was, as I was hyperventilating constantly and generally just wanted to disappear. I am lucky to have Lucas and his family around me that helped me through, but it does feel like invisible shackles where I am scared to put myself in uncomfortable situations in case I crumble again, but this time can't get through the other side. I know I am not strong enough to deal with life sometimes, so I avoid it.

I feel weak saying this, and I know that having mental health doesn't make you weak, that is old perspectives and the more people talk about it the better. It can feel like I have the weight of the world on me and worry I will crumble. A lot of my compulsions include; weight, tidiness, driving, happiness, money or anything, as soon as I get one 'compulsion' under control, another one explodes in my mind.

I want to do a further deep dive into each of my compulsions, because I can put on a happy front but everyday I struggle. At the moment eating is my biggest concern. I used to be 45kg and practically starved myself. I'd have constant headaches and tiredness but everybody said how well I looked. I've gained some weight and it is eating at me and I'm trying to get back to the unhealthy weight, but why?

I constantly think about what I eat and never allow myself to binge. I have got better in terms of not starving myself, but I do constantly obsess over what I eat. It was something me and my counsellor never got around to talking too, but I know it's something I need address.

Even since writing this, I have started another new job, I seem to change every two years. Continuing to climb the corporate ladder I got a new promotion in a company specialising in the same field, but a lot higher pay bracket and more responsibility. It is so scary adulting. It's the 'worst case scenario', the "I'm going to fail then I will never be able to work again and then I'll lose the house".

My head produces it as a live or die situation, and whilst I know that is what is happening, being in that panic zone is ghastly and alarming for anyone, let alone the person stuck in their own head. It feels like being a prisoner, but your brain is the guard who is making life worse for you. It defies all logic that our brain, who is us, can make us feel so crippled. I constantly research why this is, and I've learned a lot about the triggering of the amygdala and why our brain thinks it's a good thing to alarm us, but I have also read that constantly researching why you think certain things it counterproductive for OCD sufferers as you are pacifying the compulsion. Damned if you do, damned it you don't!

Another thing with OCD is the intrusive thoughts. What are intrusive thoughts? Intrusive thoughts seem to come out of nowhere. These thoughts and images are unwanted and often unpleasant. The content can sometimes be aggressive or sexual, or you could suddenly think about a mistake or a worry.[19] I was speaking with my therapist recently and did you know 90% of people ADMIT to having intrusive thoughts? I always question

---

[19] https://www.healthline.com/health/mental-health/intrusive-thoughts#What-are-intrusive-thoughts?

these stats, because I never get asked and nobody I know gave an answer on that or anything else so I do wonder. Like in the office for national statistics about drugs, my mum has never been asked or wouldn't admit so does it accurately catch data? Anyway I digress…

Being candid about my intrusive thoughts, I struggle really badly with them. I have suffered with them all my life, but never understood what they were. As soon as I seem to rationalise one thought, another one comes. To me, I waste so much energy trying to work out why I am thinking these and always add meaning and give weight and power to the thought, which is the worst thing to do. My therapist really opened up to me about her intrusive thoughts and said sometimes whilst driving she thinks about opening a car door on someone walking past. Of course she would never, and has never done this, but when she says it I don't think of her as crazy. But I see mine as crazy, I think they define who I am as a person. I don't remember hearing the term intrusive thoughts growing up. My intrusive thoughts always seem to get worse when I am stressed or going through change.

Being aware of intrusive thoughts is so much better though. Being able to recognise them like if you are with someone, you can almost look out for them. I feel bringing awareness to them takes the initial horrified feeling you get when you suddenly think "I could stab myself with this knife" whilst cooking. The reason you get so upset at that thought is because YOU WOULDN'T DO IT. My therapist has sent me so many useful guides on intrusive thoughts, and a good YouTube video on it "The Unwelcome Party Guest - an Acceptance & Commitment Therapy (ACT) Metaphor". [20]

It was the first Christmas in our new house and we'd just had a wall knocked out to make our living room big enough for our

---

[20] https://www.YouTube.com/watch?v=VYht-guymF4

pool table. I felt safe for the first time in my life. And that scared me. I am safe. I have never dealt with my past, I actually thought I had a normal childhood. I had clean clothes, a nice car, some sort of food, I had normal friends and none of them thought I was non-normal so everything was normal? Is that what makes it normal?

Now - I always hear people say to me 'but no families are normal'. I want to explore that. I think we use the term normal wrong. To me, normal is safe. Normal is home. Normal is feeling comfortable day to day. Normal doesn't mean that stuff doesn't happen, or people are perfect. The good, bad and the ugly is what makes the normal so normal. A crap week at work, a mum who gets in a bad mood with everyone in the house when she's in a cleaning mood, a daughter who's going through a toxic relationship, a family with an illness. These are what make us normal. So when I wanted a normal family, that's what I wanted. And that's what I now have with Lucas' family.

And nobody likes change, you have many great courses and solutions on change, such as The Change Curve. But for me, it wasn't just about the wall being removed, and I think this triggered what I now know, through counselling, is my Fawn Response.

What is the Fawn Response? The fawn response is the least known of the flight/fight/freeze but can have the biggest impact. In terms of having a fawn response, you may be ok at reacting to change and you copy well in a crisis (as you may be used to it and you do it through your subconscious), but anytime you are responsible for making a decision or creating a change that you're ultimately responsible for and it can feel paralysing. You also don't like conflict or feel you want to appease others.

I remember another time I had this 'paralysing' panic attack was when I lived at Lucas' mum and dad's and we decided to paint one of his walls a royal navy, as he had this stripped wallpaper before. We had discussed it for months and everyone was in agreement, and I was feeling lazy and decided to paint over the wallpaper as there were layers underneath and knew it would be a mammoth task. One day I was in our bedroom, and I am quite impulsive, so I decided I will paint the wall and it'll be a nice surprise for when Lucas gets home. But it didn't happen like that. I started cutting in at the top and then it set in that I am not responsible for this. I can't go back and change it if he doesn't like it. I can't wipe it off and it'll be all my fault, and by the time he came home I was breathing erratically into my arms crying because I'd thought I'd ruined his childhood room. It did pass, and we loved the colour, but that decision where everything feels down to me it is scary.

The thing with OCD is that it is different for everyone, but the term OCD has been turned into a term I get told somebody has 8 times a day at work. Whilst some of them may have it, I would love there to be some further education on what OCD really is. Yes, some people may need their phone at a 45-degree angle. But this isn't just because they like it like that, it's because if they don't they will have thoughts that something bad will happen, not just a discomfort. I know a lot of people who don't like the volume on odd numbers, again perfectly normal to avoid that as you like it on evens, but that doesn't mean you are OCD.

Even a homeless person with no property probably has a seismic routine and if it gets altered they feel disjointed. My OCD is obsessively worrying about my weight. Obsessively worrying about how I look, and it isn't because I care what others think - it is because I care about having fat. I even look at other people and look at their tummies. As soon as I quiet my mind from one issue, it feels like another one appears. One of the biggest fears for me is going on holiday because I always panic that I have left something. A sick feeling in my stomach, gut wrenching. I know a few people who have to check their passport ten times, but I do that and panic that I have left my most valuable jewellery so most of the time I never take anything of anything of value, just in case.

I don't shout my diagnosis, only to those who I value and feel I can trust. It's something I hide. I hide that I have to take two tablets a day. I have to remember to order my prescription every month and pay for it, find time to do a 20-minute walk to pick them up and queue for 10 minutes. I hate taking them everyday, panicking about going on holiday making sure I have them, or if we go abroad double check I have the right packaging so it doesn't look like I'm sneaking drugs through.

My mum is really supportive about my tablets, possibly because she self medicates too (at least mine is legal). But my dad and nan are quite old fashioned when it comes to mental health. It's always 'how's your depression'. 'Are you off your pills yet', 'too many young people are on pills'. And actually I was watching Good Morning Britain recently and they did a segment on how many young people are on antidepressants. And it made me feel like absolute crap. I HATE BEING ON THESE STUPID TABLETS. I hate that I have to remember to take them, and that I have to remember to order them before I run out, and then panic what I'm going to be like if I don't have them for a day or too. I hate having to go out and get them and remembering too. And I would much rather have that £10 a month. I'll be intrigued if someone is reading this in 10 years as they'll probably be £20 a month then! But these tablets do help me. And I have to have this internal dialogue with myself that taking medication is ok if it helps you. Like you would if you were physically ill, you need to do it if you are mentally ill too. And it does help, but I do have a nagging feeling, why is Lucas putting up with being with a 24-year-old who has had to take 2 tablets daily for over half of our relationship? I always try to put myself on a timeline as to when I should be off them, but realistically I probably will be on them for the rest of my life.

I've never called anyone out for saying oh sorry I'm just so OCD. Because why make someone else feel like crap? It is ignorance, rather than a loaded canon. It is interesting in job interviews how being seen as really OCD over things can link to good organisation. You should see my phone. I have 177 unread messages, 60 missed calls, 10 messenger notifications, 2 WhatsApp notifications. People look at my phone and go oh gosh I couldn't handle that. It doesn't bother me. They're just messages I don't need to respond to, so why open them? I think that is the big thing, I am too busy shutting up my thoughts to be clearing all these notifications. It really just doesn't matter to me.

However, one thing that will send me into a meltdown is cleanliness. If you open my sock drawers, they are not organised nicely like you see on Pinterest or Instagram, they are just shoved in there. But if you come over randomly and the floors haven't been moped I would feel like a failure. Like I had one job and I failed. I don't even care about what you may think a lot of people say 'Oh I don't mind what your house looks like'. It's not that. It's what I think of myself. I feel dirty, inadequate and a bad home owner.

This is a common stereotype with OCD, and whilst my house is tidy, the priority is clean. My boyfriend hates how untidy I can leave the room. He loves things in neat piles; so common misconceptions would put him as having OCD. But clean & tidy are different concepts. And nothing in my life is tidy, but everything is clean. I will disinfect it and it links back to my previous comments about contamination.

I am a bit cautious on mental health on social media, because sometimes it can be commercialised and glamorised. Whilst it is amazing the conversations around mental health are happening, sadly there are dark corners of the webs that exploit this and there are examples of where vulnerable people have seen this and it has had a worse effect on them.

But, there is also a lot of good. Since setting up my page, I was a bit cautious not to overshare, because I can be a little judgement on people who overshare on social media (I know, it's a bad trait, I'm working on it), or feel people do it for sympathy, or over exaggerate, but I really have tried to almost play it down, so I am not being 'click bait' or anything like that. But I have been inspired by the number of therapists and other survivors who are on the likes of Instagram sharing their experiences.

Although if you use the #mentalhealth on Instagram you will get a load of bots commenting to email an account who will charge you to promote them, even though I think only posting if you pay, rather than if their post has value doesn't sit right with me. But apart from that, the hashtags childhood trauma, PTSD all come up with really good things and I've made a lot of good connections.

Especially in terms of OCD. Online there is so much disinformation and sometimes too much 'science'. But I have seen people who are treating those with OCD, and first-hand accounts of their thoughts and feelings and it really feels like you are not alone.

My mum has always sheltered me from reality. She always had the same job, so did my step dad, and that was the only secure thing in her life, and I feel I have become scared at life, like she is. Which I know sounds ridiculous. She really does survive, not life, and whenever I ask her for advice she always says 'I don't think you can handle it' it's actually her portraying her insecurities onto me.

The more I think about how I react in life, and how I am scared does relate more to Complex Post Traumatic Stress Disorder. And for me, I've always linked this more with someone who has come back from the war or been raped or robbed. Almost one event triggers, rather than years of constant abuse. But my therapist, and again this is why getting help, although I have to pay privately, is so good, because there is so much research done on the effects childhood trauma has and the ramifications for post traumatic stress disorder and how it can even affect your brain behaviour.

Attachment trauma, also known as developmental trauma, is something we hear less about. It is when trauma occurs over time, within the context of a close relationship. It stems from psychological or physical threats (e.g. our sense of self) or emotional safety. As I mentioned earlier, my mum often says to me 'I don't think you can handle that', and I have mentioned earlier if I got another job I don't know if I'd be able to cope, these are common signs of attachment trauma, where early in life the development your capacity to cope is disrupted.

As I started this book, I promised I would tell you the truth, and nothing but the truth. I promised not to over or under dramatise, and not censor anything to try and make people look better/worse. As I've been doing a lot of research, and spent quite a lot of time reading through social media through different accounts, I've learnt quite a lot about different traumas and how the brain actually works. So as well as my obsessive compulsive order, there are quite a lot of brain reactions stemming from what happens to you as a childhood.

I have spoken just now about complex post traumatic disorder, and I'd also like to speak about relational trauma. Now, of course I am not a licensed therapist, so I'm not sure if these are all separate components or if they are an umbrella term just for trauma, so don't quote me on that. But first, I want to give a bit of science around how our brain works.

The below is from Trauma & The Brain from mediaco-op. You have three different areas of the brain:

-Reptilian; maintains bodily functions.

-Limbic System; Deals with fear & pleasure (e.g. stroke dog, dog wags tail without thinking).

-Neo Cortex; Conscious, so slower than other parts of the brain. Logical, planning and control.

Within the limbic system you have the amygdala which has one job to sense danger and 'set off the alarm'. The primitive parts of the brain override the conscious part when we sense danger. The hippocampus job is to file memories, but in times of danger it stops filing memories, which makes it harder to gather evidence later on. This system is our bodies way of protecting ourselves. The survival brain takes over the conscious brain. When trauma occurs again and again this is when the alarm system in the brain becomes jammed, and memories are stuck in the limbic system, so a trigger can set off the alarm. [21] So, I was actually in a pub with Lucas' family recently and a man walked in who reminded me of my step dad. It was his presence, his way of speaking, the way he carried himself and I just froze. I couldn't even comprehend a conversation with Lucas' family anymore and I just shut down.

Moving onto relational trauma, which is categorised by chronic abuse or neglect in childhood, often sees those who suffer interrogate themselves. They will ask things like; "am I exaggerating, was it that bad, did it really happen or have I made it up". Feeling diminished, constricted and not being able to assert yourself and trust yourself are common symptoms of relational trauma. More symptoms include feeling disconnected from your body and relationships, as well as worrying about not fitting in.

In a dream world I would love to be able to help everyone who has had a childhood trauma. And those who really want to work hard and create a new synopsis for their family, which I like to think I'm doing. So I'm trying to work so hard in my job, by writing this to hopefully one day be able to inspire and help others who aren't in the position to be helped or are being let down by the NHS.

---

[21] https://www.YouTube.com/watch?v=4-tcKYx24aA&list=PLf-3El164mtnG9ulqtSzxACRXBDFZMvp5&index=7&t=335s

Consequences Beyond Belief

Childhood trauma manifests in many different ways for various people. For my childhood trauma suffocates all feelings and all happiness. The what if's and the questioning of everyone's motivations. I always look for constant reassurance, even from those I don't value their opinion.

There are many different sources available on childhood trauma, if you know where to look, so I want anyone to read this to understand my past and hopefully get some useful information you may not have access too.

There are a key of 'core wounds' that have a lasting effect on us and they are our reaction to childhood trauma, neglect, abuse or abandonment.

The information below is from @elizabethkarinacoaching on Instagram. I will list them below and show some common signs:

- Abandonment Wound - difficulty with space, triggered easily by wounds, fears rejection and chases unavailable people in relationships

- Trust Wound - Doesn't trust themselves or anyone and doesn't open up easily. Independent and self-reliant. Takes the break of trust extremely triggering and constantly expects to be hurt and feels unsafe

- Neglect Wound - Struggles to say no and set boundaries. Fears being weak and has a lot of built-up resentment and anger. Feels overly responsible for others' emotions and fears being weak.

- Parentification Wound: Overly responsible for others and feels disconnected from emotions. Has trouble letting loose and playing. Lacks childhood memories and often picks needy partners. [22]

In all my counselling sessions (whether it be CBT or via work), one thing I always say is I hate feeling like damaged goods. And I have always tried to hide my past. But is running away from it better or worse than staring it right in the eye?

Although I've spoken a lot about my mental health, I genuinely think the reason my mother is an addict is because she's never got help. There is a saying "People in therapy are often in therapy to deal with the people in their lives who won't go to therapy". Basically, if my mum dealt with her mental health, this book wouldn't exist. And I know the stigma around mental health was different, but even now she doesn't talk. And in fact, an amazing study was done which researched the links between ADHD (Attention Deficit Hyperactivity Disorder) and opiate-dependent mothers: Ornoy, A., Finkel-Pekarsky, V., Peles, E. et al. ADHD risk alleles associated with opiate addiction: study of addicted parents and their children. Pediatr Res 80, 228–236 (2016) *"ADHD is more common in males than in females. In the children born to opiate-dependent mothers, the rate of ADHD was similarly high among males and females. This implies that intrauterine exposure to heroin, most probably increased the risk for ADHD as a result of the specific effects of heroin.... Parents addicted to opiates have a high rate of ADHD. The rate is even higher in their children, being similar in males and females. Most addicted parents carry dopamine and serotonin gene polymorphism similar to that observed in children with ADHD, even if they do not have ADHD. Hence, people carrying these genes seem to be prone to opioid addiction."*[23] I am no scientist, but to me they have identified a clear link between ADHD and opiate users, whether it is probable as a coincidence or not I am not equipped to comment.

---

[22] @Elizabethkarinacoaching - Instagram

[23] https://www.nature.com/articles/pr201678#citeas

Finding Love & Family

Growing up, I did not want to be married, nor even have a boyfriend. I think being surrounded by an abusive man tarnished my experience. Sometimes even now, when I am around certain men who share similar traits I freeze. I just think about the worst-case scenario and I just go all silent and internalise. It is great there is more awareness on domestic abuse, but sometimes men can be generalised into the same category. And I thought that, for a long time, until I met Lucas.

Love and relationships are what build us up, so it is so difficult when you've not seen good examples. I don't know anyone in my family who has not separated or is in a fully happy relationship. I swore to myself I would be a heartbreaker and never fall in love.

But I did. And luckily I did with the right person. It's very easy to go for a partner who emulates your past and you "go to what you know". Lucas is nothing like that, every day I feel I am relearning all about life. Family has been redefined, it's almost like an education. So many of my values are based on our amazing life we've built and how he's shown me what I'm worth and what I enjoy.

I have had bad experiences with the men role models in my life. But I want to focus on the positive too. He really is what every man should inspire to be. I am probably overprotective of him because I don't like to think of him knowing what I know - or feel what I felt. He doesn't deserve to know the dark side of me. He embraces all of me and is so supportive, and to know Penelope you need to know Lucas.

Everybody has a set of values they try to live beside. Whether they may be subconscious or not. In my journey to have better self-confidence and self-awareness I am really finding out my values, and those around me. I am quite an opinionated person, in fact I know what, when, how and why I want something. This doesn't mean I cannot see others' perspectives. There is a stigma around if you are opinionated you do not listen or value others' opinions. This is simply not the case, I can generally see both sides to an argument - but I believe I have strong ethical values that tilt me a certain way.

A big value of mine is cleanliness. I know what this stems from. As I've said before, we did live in a clean home. However, all of our spoons were brown. Like tea stained beyond belief. I would scrub them routinely. Soak them in bleach. I was always so embarrassed of anyone using our spoons and always blaming it on the fact we didn't have a dishwasher and my mum left the spoons in a tea bag holder with used tea bags.

I recently told a friend of mine, and she actually opened up about her estranged father being an alcoholic all of her life. But she said my actions make sense. She recalled a story where we were at a close friend's BBQ, and when they bought the cutlery out she said I was inspecting it asking how it had been washed. (I have developed a dishwasher vs hand washing dilemma. Growing up I never had a dishwasher so I associate hand washing with my house and feel dirty. I know they can be as clean but that is just my experience) They all had a bit of a laugh and were calling me a snob in a light hearted way. I took no offence but it was interesting she recalled that and linked the reasoning once she knew my story.

As I mentioned earlier, I had gone to an Al-Anon group. It was good. They gave me this book Hope For Today which covered a lot of good things, although a lot was incomparable as it is for family and friends of alcohol users, and there are some notable differences. The main thing I actually couldn't relate too is the God references.

I love that people like to follow or believe in something. In the same way Lucas and I follow Liverpool is similar to a religion. It's the sense of belonging. The sense of purpose. However, I have always found it really hard to believe there's a god out there. As I talked about earlier, I grew up around Jehovah's Witnesses and I did history at school too. So many people use religion for a reason for hate and I just don't see if there was a god why they wouldn't stop all of this. Why wouldn't they stop addicts and dealers? Maybe I'm angry at the world and if I met 'God' I'd like to sit him down and ask him how the hell it's ok to allow so much horror to happen. Good people with the ability to stop evil should. If you believe in God, I am pleased you have your sense of protection.

For me I have always questioned what makes a house a home? Only now do I truly know the answer. Safety and love. Now let me take you into my experience of living with a high functioning addict. Growing up, I lived in many houses and flats as discussed earlier. We ended up in a standard house (2 up, 2 down sort of thing). From the outside looking in, it was a modest family home, with my mum and step dad owning it.

Our house was always tidy, but it was not clean. I never really went into my mother's room, but if I did, I would see the bed strategically moved to cover the blood splatter from their injection. You'd see their night stands covered in burnt spoons and needles. The look of sheer panic on their faces whenever I went into their room was a picture. Their bedding would always have blood splatters across, the same as near the toilet and the toilet bin would be full of blood splattered tissue. I don't think I ever slept or napped in that room with my mum. My sister went through a stage of terrible nightmares and she was banned from coming in, probably because she would have gotten in the way of their use.

When the house was full, the living room would be overrun with the two zombies sprawled out across the sofas like flattened roadkill. They would pass out as soon as they had their fixes for hours, whilst having something like MOTO GP on in the background for my step dad. They would get up, roll a cigarette on one of the side tables and in their narcosis state scurry, outside to come back in to pass out. They would leave tobacco everywhere around the house. I would never drink or eat at their tables as they were covered in tobacco.

The kitchen was the least used room in the house, apart from mother making cups of tea. There was never really any washing up as they did not eat, and they would just reuse the same mug and glass for days on end. The fridge only consisted of chocolate, cheese, butter and milk. Especially Cadbury Mini Roll's that now trigger me every time I see them. There was never any raw food or salad, which I remember being amazed at when I went to Lucas' parents house. Their array was like being at a supermarket.

In the cupboards there was expired flour, baking kits and anything you had to put effort into. We would normally have crisps, stale cereal and a ton of super noodles. There was no ambition for anything in the cupboards to be cleaned or look good. We had random plates, bowls and cutlery. The cutlery housed their spare tobacco so you'd often find the little brown curly bits in between the cutlery drawers and the odd filter on your spoon.

When I got old enough, I started asking for birthdays and Christmas' to decorate the house. When I turned 18 and got a full-time job I just decorated some of the rooms myself.

A big part of my personality is the 'all or nothing' thinking. And this is not exclusive to obsessive compulsive disorder. I have taken the following description from Dr Julie's 'Why Did Nobody Tell Me This Before', this I highly recommend. I don't really read as I struggle to stick with anything, or I skip pages because I get bored, but this is great, it's almost like a bible that I sometimes (when I remember) go back and have a look at. This is not a paid advertisement by the way!

All-or-nothing thinking. Also known as black-and-white thinking, this is another thought bias that can make mood worse if we leave it unchecked. This is when we think in absolutes or extremes, *I am either a success or a complete failure. If I don't look perfect, I'm ugly. If I make a mistake, I should never have bothered.* This polarised thinking style leaves no room for the grey areas that are often closer to reality. The reason this pattern of thought makes everything harder is because it makes us vulnerable to more intense emotional reactions. If failing one exam means you are a failure as a person, then the emotional fallout from that will be more extreme and much harder to pull back from. When you feel low in mood, you're more likely to think in this polarised way. But it's important to remember that this is not because your brain is getting things wrong or malfunctioning in any way. When we are under stress, all-or-nothing thinking creates a sense of certainty or predictability about the world. What we then miss is the chance to think things through more logically, weighing up the different sides of the argument and coming to a more informed judgement.[24]

I remember first reading that and it was almost like she was sitting in my head. And it is important to remember that with anything, bringing awareness is so important, but it doesn't mean you will just stop. I know I do this thinking pattern, and I try to bring awareness to it, but if I don't they ruminate. I must drive my partner mad because everything has to be done in a certain way, everything has to be clean otherwise I think we are terrible homeowners and don't deserve a house. It's like when people come round if I don't feed them or offer them a drink I don't deserve to host.

When you think of values you can also relate them to a set of rules you live by. I always feel there is a right or wrong way. And don't get me wrong, that doesn't mean I can't see both sides of an argument, I was always told I would make a great politician as I can argue either side or something with whole hearted passion.

---

[24] Why Did Nobody Tell Me This Before, Dr Julie, p26

As well as right and wrong, it is good and bad. I categorise my family into these, and I can't have them in the middle. Yes we all have our bad and good qualities, and that's what makes us human. But I judge those on the facts and then it tips the scale one way or another, for example, take my mother. She was always good until recently, but now she is bad. But when she went to rehab I felt she had to be good, so then she moved, then when she relapsed and lied she went back to bad.

Now life is full of grey areas, so this is not really a rational way of thinking. As in Dr Julie's extract, all-or-nothing thinking can be linked to us trying to make sense of clarity. Having a sense of certainty can make you feel comfortable, but life is full of uncertainties. One thing all-or-nothing gives is a full sense of certainty when you have such strong values. For example, you know if you always react a certain way to a situation, then you can be more certain around the outcome.

In this book it also talks all about anxiety around death. 'Dr Julie's - Why Did Nobody Tell Me This Before'. It sounds really morbid, but it is good food for thought. Life is precious, which maybe feeds back to why I feel guilty about feeling a strained relationship with my mum. Ultimately even when we die we want our values we lived throughout our lives to be honoured and respected, don't we? There are two activities linked to this chapter the first being -

What would people say about you at your funeral?

Try telling yourself how good you are, like you'd talk about someone else. So I've tried myself and I wrote how 'she' is, and they were complimentary (in my opinion) but I deleted/erased it because I didn't feel comfortable seeing them. I do want to try it again, but I feel like I'm wanting for reassurance it'll be ok and somebody tell me to do it. Which takes me on to activity two.

What is your mantra?

What would I have written on my grave stone?

Considering I live 10 metres from a graveyard and do spend time reading them (I hope I do this in a way to humble my living?), I should have some inspiration. I know they're normally regal, or quotes from the bible. But as I've stated I do not believe in religion so it would need me to 'advertise' a quotation from a holy book. I guess I could look up some food quotes, and I've found a lot via Instagram. But 'key messages' I am thinking of being featured would be about loving hard - but only those who are worthy.

I never really had any boyfriends growing up. Lucas and I were each others first relationship's. Even though I was a popular girl in school and wore make up and was extremely social I was the only one out of my friends who didn't constantly have boyfriends. I hadn't even really kissed one.

When Lucas and I first started speaking, I already had in my head it wouldn't go anywhere. I had decided he probably thought I was some slag. I knew he was a few years older, so I had assumed he just wanted to sleep with me. I wasn't scared of the world when I met him. I wasn't scared of actions and did not appreciate the consequences.

I remember even falling in love with the little things with him, like his smell and his amazingly long eyelashes. He showered everyday, which from someone who had just about a borderline functioning bath it was impressive. He would never not brush his teeth, and his standards were just fascinating. I remember first going into his bedroom, expecting to see a late boys' teens room like I normally had, you know, dirty sheets, smelly clothes, terrible decoration. No. This wasn't like that. It was intentionally simplistic yet functional for a teenager boy. He had his PlayStation set up and he had a touch of Liverpool memorabilia without it looking like he was a 5-year-old.

I used to dress, and I'm thinking of a way not to insult myself, but inappropriate. Not in the way I'd have everything showing, but it was about timing and suitability. For example, when we first started dating I went to one of his football matches in a freezing amble January. Everybody else was in their thermals, scarves and boots. Not me. I dressed in leather trousers, heeled boots and a fashionable and NOT warm jacket, emphasis on the NOT warm.

I felt like I was learning all about life whilst we were embedded in our relationship together. Not only about myself, and how much I loved being hygienic and the finer things, but also about family life. In the common age it is very common to eat on the sofa, but given I barely even had cooked meals on the regular, to even sit on a dining table together would feel unnatural. So to rejoin every evening and discuss our days and help set and clean up the table was so enjoyable for me. Not the cleaning up, but just being a part of something.

We have all been guilty of watching a film or series like The Notebook and wanting that crippling, to die for love. But in this day of age, if you are really intense with something it can be seen as negative. Lucas is my soulmate, my life partner, my yin to my yan. I love him so much and he loves me. Sometimes it hurts how much I love him. I want to protect him at all costs. I was 16 when we met, and he stuck by me through my OCD diagnosis, my inability to get out of bed, my life story, my wobbles.

In a happy, fairytale relationship with my Amore Della Mia Vita (Lucas, He will feature a lot later in the happy days). The best way to think about us is to listen to Iron & Wine, Flightless Bird, American Mouth. It is a very comforting and subtle song. Perfectly not perfect. He is the reason why I want to help others, and why I have the strength too. I was always very selfish before him, but he taught me the value of love, family and compassion and he makes me want to be a better person. We have been together over 8 years and I love growing with him.

I actually went to school with Lucas' younger sister for a few years, and Lucas was in my sister's year at school, although they didn't really talk. I went to a lot of schools in my life as mentioned before, so when I left my first secondary school I left Lucas' sister behind and hadn't seen her in years. One of my best friends growing up lived 5 down doors from me and still went to the same school, so when it came to picking college, I went back to that school's sixth form to everyone's surprise. Lucas's sister had gone to the local college so I didn't see her. Lucas randomly Instagram messaged me and we met and just hit it off. I had crazy anxiety but I just went with it and the rest is history.

Now things haven't always been easy. I lied to him for the first couple of months why I didn't want him to come over. I said my room was being redecorated, but I assume you know the real reason by now. We spent the first few months just at his house, and it was quite a big adjustment period. I also was really fussy at eating because I didn't have the opportunity to try a lot. I still am a fussy eater, but I have opened my palette up a lot more. When Lucas's mum used to make spaghetti bolognese, I wouldn't admit that I didn't like mince and would just eat it, and I'd get so nervous about eating with them all I would go and be sick in their bathroom. I never told them until a lot later.

I was also a very different person when I met Lucas, I socially smoked, drank like a fish and had just stopped smoking weed. I cared more about my image on social media than real life, and I still had the mantra 'It's not about how you feel it's how you look'. So I had a big group of friends, most of them I didn't really like, and their fakeness showed. As soon as I stopped drinking as much and wasn't as available and they slowly all fell off.

Lucas' sister was in an abusive relationship that even ended up in court, and although she had a nice and new boyfriend I felt they were quite reluctant with me. They did welcome me with open arms, but they did like me to go home and not stay too much. Especially when I went through my breakdown. Although he stood by my side every step of the way.

We were young, and it is rare to stay with the person you are with when you are now these days, we are all caught in whirlwind romances and social media dating, so perhaps wanting to keep it not to serious at first is a good way to be.

He is the old-fashioned true love. He truly looks after me and always has my best intentions. And the love is very clearly reciprocated. We do really bring out the best in each other, whilst he has helped me and took me with all my baggage, he constantly says I motivate him, for example he didn't drive when we met and then he did and he's gone from strength to strength in his career (but of course there are more important things), and he says I have really helped him through his struggles.

Like I said earlier we now have our dream house together. But I actually think the safety and happiness of finally having a space to call my own was the catalyst of discovering this was the first time I'd ever fully felt safe in my life. So I am currently in therapy. Luckily, my work offers counselling sessions for free. The NHS waiting list was 6-8 weeks and when I was at my worst I couldn't wait. I have stopped the counselling because it ended up just me talking about my childhood again and again, and it felt like I was stuck in a loop, so I invested in some private Cognitive Behavioural Therapy courses, on the back of a really inspiring podcast on how the woman had coped with her thoughts. I've always just shut them up, not cured them as such. The CBT is really helping in processing my thoughts and it is worth it, and it's made me want to make sure other people going through something similar, who can't afford it, can access it, and this is my new mission statement.

I know I am very lucky that I can afford to do this, but there is a massive gap, especially when I was in school/sixth form where I didn't have the money to do this. And really without it you feel you are surviving and not living. This is why I want to help others. I did Psychology at A-Level before sixth form asked me to leave, and I loved it, because I find it all so interesting.

But sometimes my scars do show. I do react differently to others in situations and I cannot control my emotions. You wouldn't know I had trauma day to day, but when anything happens I recently said to Lucas that it's like sometimes it feels they are a complete dinner set (few scratches, like everybody has), and I am the deformed tea pot. Sometimes I fit in, and others my tea spills and I cannot control it.

It isn't anybody's business to know my story, but I also feel like you get me so much more when you know the real me. Without that I seem an arrogant, opinionated and successful person. I'm not very well liked, because I can't do small talk or fake feelings.

Lucas' family and Lucas have given me a whole new hope for living. Gosh I've fought like cats and dogs with all of them but they have helped me. You know some days when you just want to cry? There are the people that make it all ok. When I think about my future and my wedding with Lucas, I don't see my mum in the pictures. I see Lucas's mum. I see Lucas's mum crying when she sees me in *the* dress. I even want her to stay with me the night before instead of Lucas and she'll help me keep calm more than anyone else. I couldn't think of better people to help raise my imaginary children.

To know Penelope Red is to understand Lucas too. There is no Penelope without Lucas behind the scenes being my cheerleader. He is extremely empathetic and sensitive. I will hate when he reads this, because reading my harrowing stories will destroy him. He hates what I went through and it makes him feel all types of ways. I sometimes don't tell him certain stories because it won't do any good, it will just upset him.

And it really is true that right now you might be in a situation that you think you won't survive, but six months ago you were in a situation that you didn't think you'd survive, and two years before that you were in a situation you didn't think you'd survive and the point is you will always surprise yourself and you will always make it through.

The Now

There is a saying that I really live by at the moment - I'm healthy but I'm not well. We all know health is wealth, and I am healthy. When I think of 'healthy' I think of physical fitness. My blood pressure is average, I'm not under or overweight, ok yes I do over analyse my weight, but nothing the doctor would diagnose as physically wrong, but all together I never don't often go to the doctors with pain etc. (although with the current state of the NHS, you can't get an appointment for 2-3 weeks, by that time you're fine. But when I think of 'well', I think of mental wellness. I feel weaker than other people, like I am easily breakable and more vulnerable. Although if you met me I don't think you'd think that. I overcompensate in my head about being a failure by pushing myself to the best I can be, even if it's achievable or not healthy. I struggle with perfectionism and often just feel I let myself and everyone else down around me. Perfectionism is so draining.

I've never really had any self-esteem. There are a few things I am proud of about myself, such as how clean my house is (once I've just cleaned), my clothes, my hair. And I love my honesty, even if people cringe at what I'm about to say. It quite makes me laugh how people are so concerned about what I will say next. I have been working on that, but then that's what makes me, me right?

I went to a family and friends addiction group after my mum got out of rehab. I'm not supposed to talk about what happened there so I won't share their stories. But the general theme I picked up was that family and friends of loved ones who are in an addiction, whether it is alcohol or drugs, always seem to doubt themselves, doubt their thoughts, their decisions, their kindness. That's something I have always struggled with.

'In the past I focused on anyone but myself - my husband, my children, my friends. I scurried around trying to meet what I perceived to be their needs, trying to make their lives orderly, comfortable, safe and secure. I didn't see that I was still trying to control the disorder, discomfort and lack of safety and security of my own childhood'.[25] This is an extract from the Al-Anon's book 'Hope For Today' that they kindly gave me for free. A lot of it isn't relevant due to the alcoholism parts, however this statement feels like I could have written this.

I try to control everything. I am not controlling in terms of who Lucas sees or anything, but controlling of looking after him. I feel if I don't do him dinner, or keep the home nice I am not good enough. That is in no way a reflection of how he thinks or how he makes me feel. He is so grateful and thankful and doesn't expect any of this from me and constantly tells me I don't have to do it. I also have to control things like driving anywhere, or booking a holiday or transport. Even with driving, it isn't just me being the driver, it's being in control of the car, for example with a train or bus I cannot control how or when we stop like I could if I was in control of a vehicle. It suits my job quite well as I do a lot of driving, but allowing myself to consistently have control can be counterproductive as it feeds my unhealthy obsessions.

I psychoanalyse everything. I struggled at school with that. If my friends and I were having a bitch session about a friend, I couldn't then go over and be really friendly with the person we've just spoken about. It just isn't a part of my nature. I would feel like an untrue and bad person. Actually, everybody does it, and it has prevented me from having long-life friends. I put so much pressure on myself to be true to my word and my values, that I work against myself.

I have been realising a lot of what I've been feeling is common for friends/family of those who are addicts/users. As I said earlier, you can't find that much on heroin. I used to wish she

---

[25] Hope For Today, February 8, p38

was an alcoholic as there was more help for that. And where you can legally buy alcohol, it isn't a crime as such. But my mum is an addict, and a criminal. As a child when you think of a criminal you think of 'lock up and throw away the key'. I had seen my mother's old boyfriend in and out of jail, and didn't want my mum to be sent to jail or lose her job. I knew if either of the above happened my mum's life would be over as such.

Of course, I don't wish for anyone to be an alcoholic and know there are unique problems with alcoholism. I never had to worry about my mum stumbling down the street, or picking me up half dressed.

Heroin seems to be a taboo as if we were in Harry Potter and 'he shall not be named'. When I would come home from school I would google 'child of an addict', or 'heroin addicts' and the information was so sparse. The stories on heroin only seem to concentrate on the homeless and unemployed who get mixed up in petty crime, but my mum didn't fit in that bracket so I had no support or guidance. Society almost acts as if you can't be a high functioning heroin addict.

Please. Do. Better.

Please can everybody all agree we ALL have a duty for safeguarding.

Please can everybody agree to stop writing troubled kids off without looking into what happened to them – not what's wrong with them.

I still have my struggles, but I now know I am not alone in what I faced. Since openly talking about my experience throughout my childhood (within the safety of Instagram without my family knowing) I have had so many messages including somebody saying they can sleep better knowing they are not alone in what they have been through. Any child of an addicted parent needs to be seen and heard.

But there is light, and there are tools I've learned that I wish I knew earlier.

The biggest thing I learned was the three C's of supporting someone with addiction.

> *I did not **cause** it*
>
> *I can not **cure** it*
>
> *I am not in **control** of it*

But I want to add one to this. A Penelope Red twist shall we call it.

*A **child** should never feel responsible for their parents actions.*

Not quite as snappy as the others, but I feel so strongly that a child should not bear that much responsibility. I know how that feels.

So I want to give you a full update of where I am, how my mum is and what our relationship is like. As mentioned earlier, I had a mental blip last Christmas (2021). My mum got a rescue dog and it seemed to trigger my own childhood. Seeing her looking after a vulnerable helpless dog reminded me of her looking after, or should I say not looking after us. I have gone into how this came about but this is where I am at. I stopped speaking to my mum to give myself a break.

It was really hard to cut the initial communications from my mum, but it really did me so well. I am speaking to her again and falling back into my parenting habits, but whilst and to quote friends 'we were on a break', I really grieved for my childhood and had realised how I had childhood trauma and I didn't even know.

My mum also didn't respect the space. I remember just stopping texting her and would be a little bit more blunt, and then I just said to her that I'm healing at the moment, and while I love her, I needed space. I needed to work out whilst I felt numb. She was actually really good, of course she was upset, but she said it may take time but she will be there once I've resolved in my head.

That lasted about 2 weeks then she started trying to contact me again and then texting me 'I guess you're not ready yet', and saying I know it may take a year, and putting timelines on something she cannot guide. I just felt under pressure to sort it. My whole family was on my back (my sister, nan, uncle), to 'get over it'. My sister especially was quite toxic throughout the whole situation.

It's always 'but that's your mum'. Yes, but she didn't protect me as she should, and it felt like nobody was allowing me to validate my experience or feel anything. I read a really good book by Dr Julie - Why Did Nobody Tell Me This Before, that goes into grief and what we know about it. And I realised I was going through the cycle of grief. I had been sad, but at this point I was really angry. Like really angry. How dare my mum do this to my sister and I? How dare my step dad lay a finger on any of us?

I had moments thinking it would be better if she did just overdose. And I feel so evil writing that, and I do not want her to die at all, and some of you may read that and go, you are a psycho, but I want to be really honest with you. I feel like it is inevitable, like all the statistics and studies show that heroin addicts generally do die from an overdose. I believe she doesn't want to get clean. She only says it to pacify my sister & I, or to shut us up.

But the truth is, it's come to the point, I think I accept her for being a heroin addict. I have thought long and hard about what my mum being sober would look like, but that day realistically won't come. I don't even think my mum would be happy sober. Heroin is her one true love, and to her she functions fine on it, it's us that have the problem with it, not her. Although she detests this, I feel like she doesn't know a world without drugs and I don't know if she'd even be happy sober. This has been her life for over half her life.

When I started counselling and started deep diving into what really happened in my childhood, I realised it wasn't normal. At the age of 23 (At the time), that is scary to start recalling memories you'd buried deeper than the oceans floor. I remember my counsellor asked me to draw a timeline of my life. And pick out any happy memories. All of my teenage years I'd forgotten. I can remember school, and my friends, getting the bus into town but nothing else. That's when I really started to remember the memories.

I do, regrettably, associate my mum with being the spider web of most of my problems. I know I am an adult, and I have to take responsibility for my actions and my future but I can't help feeling like my struggles are due to her being a negligent mother. Like the way I am always in fight or flight mode. Or the fact I constantly feel I need to ring her and check in, to check she hasn't overdosed or doesn't feel alone and go back to my step dad (which she does anyway).

I still feel so much shame and guilt over my mum's addiction, and although, like my sister, just moving on and not letting it affect my future is probably the 'textbook' way of dealing with it, I just feel like I have to get this off my chest, like I have to analyse why this happened and why it happened to me. I really feel like there must be a reason it happened to me, otherwise, I feel like I must have deserved it.

Whilst writing this, she actually took voluntary redundancy, which is really stressful. Hopefully by the time you are reading this she has got a new job, which I am hopeful off because career wise, she is great and has a lot to offer, but more importantly an unemployed addict is never good. She has also just had a massive pay off, due to her being there since I was young, and the thought of her having all that money is absolutely terrifying. I did say to her it could be a good idea to put it in a bank account where she needs my sister or I as a secondary signature if she wants a large purchase, to deter her from dipping into it too much, or even if she has an accountant look after it.

Prior to her taking redundancy she went on a cruise. Since rehab she asked to be taken off the methadone prescription, and my mum is too proud to go back and be asked to go and be put back on it (So I thought she was on pure heroin). Due to not having methadone, when she went on a cruise, (which she said was with a friend but was probably Neil), she told me she was taking codeine instead as a substitute, which as we know has its own problems.

From her being back from her cruise and her now being unemployed, she has talked about going back to rehab, and that she wants to change, basically her usual script. A couple of weeks ago she told me she had pain like she had from her kidney stones before, and I just had a terrible feeling.

The next day I was in a nearby town with Lucas' mum having brunch (her and I have THE best days out together), when I got a text. It said

"I'm in hospital".

Calling - No Answer Repeats x10

That's the extent of the text, so of course I am panicking. My mind races to all the possibilities, has she FINALLY overdosed? Is it due to her just doing pure heroin now? After trying to call her and her not picking up, she does eventually tell me it is her kidney stones and she said don't worry about coming home to see her dog as her neighbour was popping round and feeding her and she thought she'd go home later.

So I decided I needed to go and see her, she sounded like death. I know I needed to speak to the doctors, because there is no truth with my mother. Lucas came with me, and I tried the NHS switchboard 100 times to find out what ward she was in but got no luck, so we just went to reception and they told me her ward.

We went up and there she was in a wheelchair being escorted back to wait in a crowded waiting room, with her in excruciating pain. It broke my heart. I spoke to the nurse and said my mum is in so much pain can't she lay down? And they had no beds. I can't even tell you how inhumane it made me feel, let alone my mum. But we can talk about the under-resourcing and failures of the NHS in a whole other book series, which I'm sure has been done.

I asked to speak to a doctor, and I said to them "you do know she's a heroin addict, right?" in which they looked shocked and said no (my mum rang me later to thank me for telling them, as she didn't). They must not have looked at her records, although I don't even know if that comes up or if it's on her records I don't know, I don't work in healthcare. I also told them she was off the methadone and on straight heroin so I wanted them to know everything in case they gave her any medication that could react. They said they'd also get the drug nurse to go and see her which I was really impressed with, thank you Doctor.

They confirmed it was kidney stones and she had been given medication after her last surgery to remove previous kidney stones to stop them returning, in which she admitted to not taking. As I walked back into the waiting room/triage area, my mum panicked and got off the phone. In that moment I knew it was my step dad. The one she 'doesn't talk too or ever see'. I asked who it was, where she had clearly concocted a lie about her neighbour asking where the key is to feed her dog (although she told me her neighbour had gone round earlier, so surely she would have already found the key?) I know I am Sherlock Holmes, you become a great detective and question everything when your parents are compulsive liars.

My sister doesn't work Fridays, due to her salary being substantial enough in medicine, so she normally comes home Thursday nights to see her boyfriend who lives near us, so I rang her and told her about mum and that mum may need to stay overnight, in which she said yeah I'll come home tonight. I thought, great, all sorted. How I was wrong.

Later that evening, I got a call from my sister saying she needs to go 'in work' the next day so could I get her from the station tomorrow, in which I said ok, so I said I would have the dog that night. I called my mum and said look I'm heading over to yours, but I will not go in if my step dad's there tell me straight, and she admitted it was him on the phone, and it was him that was looking after her dog that day, but he would not be there on my arrival.

What did I do once I got there? I start going through her bins. I go through her drawers and boxes back like I was a teenager. I know it is my choice to do it, but I feel driven too, because it's the only way I get the truth. I found loads of methadone, so I had just told the doctor misinformation that she was off it when actually she was buying it off the street (who even does that), I found boxes on boxes on codeine so now I'm concerned she's addicted to that as well, and I found loads of receipts of purchases she's made and missed appointments she told me she'd attended. The deadliest blow, the beer cans in the recycling bin. They brought back so many horrific memories. My mum does not drink, and I knew exactly who they were, so again another lie. Even when I confronted my mum about it she pretended to be annoyed 'what he must have done when he went and fed my dog, the cheek of it'. Yeah, yeah mum whatever.

I called my sister to tell her what had happened, and oh guess what she's out. That's why she couldn't come home. Even though I had work early the next day and was running around mum in the hospital, she didn't come home because she wanted to go and get hammered. Thanks sis.

My mum ended up staying nearly a week, and she asked me to take her some essentials and buy some new PJs and a dressing gown as the ones at home had holes in them from her dog, which I did. When I got in she just told me how she's finally had *the* realising she doesn't want this for her life. She was saying how she had felt the time in there provided her the space and clarity she needed to reevaluate. She talked about volunteering, now she is out of work and giving back to the world.

Once she was out, my auntie went round to return her dog and to check on my mum, and then rang me as she wanted to say what a wonderful and positive time she had with my mum. My auntie is quite new to this saga, and her ignorance is easy to see, although I am guilty of being the same. I am very grateful for her taking her time out of her life to go and sit with my mum and try and help her. She isn't blood, she is my dad's brother's ex wife, so the fact she is still trying with my mum is going above and beyond. It was only because my nan told everyone about my mum's addiction as she can't keep a secret (she even told a taxi driver who happened to know my dad and asked her in which my dad denied, as my mum could lose her job if this becomes common knowledge).

My auntie was very optimistic and had said how motivated my mum seemed, and how she was clear on how she didn't even enjoy using the heroin and she wanted this monkey off her back as the saying goes. Of course, I didn't want to seem ungrateful for my auntie's care so I entertained this new 'epiphany'. However, I did say, this is all great BUT I have heard this before. My auntie went on to protest that this is different. My auntie said they had made a new arrangement that every time she wanted to use she'd call my auntie or go over to see her. That definitely has not happened, and if drug rehabilitation was that easy I think we wouldn't have the drug crisis we do, but I do appreciate her enthusiasm and her determination to help my mum, but you can't help someone who doesn't help themselves. It took me back to when I believed everything my mother said, I could hear the hope and optimism in her voice, just like what used to be in mine.

My auntie also said my mum was not going to be returning to rehab as she was put on this new drug you put under your tongue, and even if you do take heroin it doesn't work. As soon as I got off the phone to her I had to google this. Why haven't I heard of it before? I did think my mum had made it up, because why hasn't she done it before? But she wasn't lying, this is a real thing. I have found various information about this drug, with its name being Buprenorphine. Buprenorphine is an opioid medication. "Buprenorphine sublingual tablets (given under the tongue) are a prescription medicine used to treat **opioid addiction (either prescription or illegal drugs), as part of a complete treatment program that also includes counseling and behavioral therapy.**" [26]

So, my mum isn't having counselling or behavioural therapy, and from what I can assume is that you have to continue to put it under your tongue for it too work, which I doubt my mum is keeping up with. Part of me is wondering why my mum and I haven't discussed this earlier, or why it isn't as talked about as methadone.

But I am continuing to knock on doors. I have written to Kensington Palace, I have had meetings with Mind, Aid, NSPCC and whatever addiction charity you can think of.

But the biggest part of my journey is how much I've learned through starting my Instagram page. I am not trying to advertise, but if you do want to follow please do. Whilst the world is full of prejudices and bias, the one thing that doesn't care is addiction.

Addiction does not care who you are. Parent, child, grandparent, doctor, nurse, lawyer or shop assistant. Addiction from drug, alcohol and gambling affects all communities, countries, ages, backgrounds, socio-economics and beliefs. Whilst we all try to be

---

[26] https://www.drugs.com/buprenorphine.html

more diverse and inclusive it is a shame the only thing that is such a horrible disease. And I still do not agree with the term 'high functioning'. I get why we call it a high functioning addict, but it gives a false perception of a positive experience. Yes, it was better that we had a warm house and we're able to buy clothes BUT behind close doors she still displayed the same behaviours of ANY addict:

- Not cuddling me, physically shying away from contact
- Pass out all weekend like a zombie
- Never come to parents evening or show an interest in school etc.
- Never knowing or caring what's going on in my life

I too still see my mum as a glitch or an anomaly but the fact is she isn't. There are so many people in my position. I have had some amazing messages over the last few days and I promise to continue to post my experiences, my lessons learned and continue to not knock but bang on doors.

It is who I want to be, and how I want to influence others. I strive to be a really good person. I want to care for Lucas and give him the best life, because that is what he deserves. I want to have a life I am proud of and I want to give those around me the opportunities I missed out on, but also to give myself opportunities.

For me, I have always felt my experience has had to mean something, as I've spoken too. And I saw this beautifully poetic quote which I think sums up how I am seeing this opportunity. "Sometimes when in a dark place you think you've been buried when actually you've been planted" Christine Caine.

Life sucks, right? But we have two choices. Feel sorry for ourselves or look at the opportunity it's given us. I am sick of feeling sorry for my mum for her knock backs, but really she could have turned them into building blocks. It's easier said than done, but I really need my experience to be a planter for me. I want to lay foundations and question our stereotypes on addicts.

It's really hard to be optimistic, but everything happens for a reason… Right?

I was recently featured on Shaun Attwood's YouTube channel. He's kind of a big podcaster on YouTube. His channel is a true crime one, but his amazing co-host Jen Hopkins and I did a show talking about my story. But it's interesting I was so scared about the backlash I was going to get. I have spoken before about 'not having it bad enough' or 'people have it worse', and I think that is what goes through a lot of our minds before we tell our stories. But I want to tell you every story is important. Just because someone's type of trauma is your type of normal doesn't mean it's okay. There is a saying that there is no greater agony than bearing an untold story inside of you.

I have needed to look at myself in the mirror, because although my mum's addiction caused me to be responsible for her, she can't not stop me from feeling that way. Only I can control how I react and handle my feelings.

Two months ago I would NOT have been able to say that, as I blamed my mum for everything, when really I need to decide how I react to situations.

I know my mum likes me to parent her, but also by me parenting her it's not helping her like I think it is, and it's not helping me. I try to remember that taking responsibility for somebody else means you're also taking the responsibility away from them.

I really am on a journey to see how I get to a new normal with my mum being a heroin addict where it doesn't consume me.

I have been thinking about where to finish this. Where do I end the chaos and every day change? And in this I guess I had hoped by writing this I would be fully healed, but healing is a never-ending journey. It does get better, but life does remind you of our pasts and our minds can play tricks on us.

So let's end on this topic - writing. Since writing this and my various articles for the fostering magazine and The Mix I've realised I enjoy literacy. It was the only subject I was actually ever really good at in school and didn't really have to try. If I tried I could have been a lot better. But on social media I've seen such beautiful poems. I've tried to write one, but I just can't get started. Then the other night I was watching a new South Park episode (which is one of my favourites), and they were talking about ChatGPT. I've never heard of this, so my partner explained what it was and set up an account. Basically it is artificial intelligence that can give you information and respond to messages and type CVs for you. It can literally do everything. It's quite scary. But I asked the software to write a poem on children of addicts and it is incredibly beautiful and thought provoking. I really wanted to share it:

"The Children Of Addiction
In their eyes, a pain that's deep,
A silent sorrow that they keep,

Their parents lost in a haze.
A world of drugs, a deadly craze,
The children watch as days go by,

As their parents live and die.
They see the highs and lows they take,

And the endless promises they break.
Their innocence lost to the streets,

A childhood shattered at their feet.
With every hit and every score,

Their hearts break a little more.
Yet still they hope and still they dream,
Of a life that's different,

A life that's clean.
A life without the pain they know,
A life where love can truly grow.

So let us not forget these souls,
Whose lives have been consumed by holes.

Let us offer love and care,
And show them that we're always there."[27]

---

[27] www.chatgpt.com

Appendix

This book is highly derived from research via books, social media and different studies that have been conducted. Below is a full list of all referenced works for further reading.

- https://www.renewallodge.com/are-you-a-high-functioning-drug-addict/
- https://americanaddictioncenters.org/methadone-addiction/and-mixing-heroin
- https://www.hopkinsmedicine.org/health/treatment-tests-and-therapies/opioids
- heroin meaning - Google search
- https://alcoholchange.org.uk/alcohol-facts/fact-sheets/alcohol-statistics
- https://www.ncbi.nlm.nih.gov/pmc/articles/PMC5007563/#:~:text=Overall%2C%20the%201960s%20and%201970s,condensed%20this%20attitude%20against%20psychiatry.
- https://www.childrenscommissioner.gov.uk/chldrn/
- https://www.gov.uk/government/publications/parents-with-alcohol-and-drug-problems-support-resources/parents-with-alcohol-and-drug-problems-guidance-for-adult-treatment-and-children-and-family-services
- https://draxe.com/health/self-sabotaging/
- @jeanpyschologist Instagram
- https://www.choosingtherapy.com/emotional-incest/
- https://www.kvg.org

- Dr Perry & Oprah Winfrey - 'What Happened To You?'
- Dr Julie - 'Why Did Nobody Tell Me This Before?'
- https://www.instagram.com/p/CpmkZ_kqybe/
- https://www.talktofrank.com/drug/heroin
- https://www.oxfordreference.com/display/10.1093/acref/9780199534067.001.0001/acref-9780199534067-e-8554;jsessionid=D913C5C0E55C3737598CBEDF864D5719
- https://www.independent.co.uk/news/education/education-news/private-school-pupils-drug-alcohol-addictions-more-likely-new-research-money-fake-id-a7766951.html
- https://www.mind.org.uk/information-support/types-of-mental-health-problems/obsessive-compulsive-disorder-ocd/about-ocd/
- https://www.healthline.com/health/mental-health/intrusive-thoughts#What-are-intrusive-thoughts?
- https://www.YouTube.com/watch?v=VYht-guymF4
- https://www.YouTube.com/watch?v=4-tcKYx24aA&list=PLf-3El164mtnG9ulqtSzxACRXBDFZMvp5&index=7&t=335s
- @Elizabethkarinacoaching - Instagram
- https://www.nature.com/articles/pr201678#citeas
- Al-Anon - 'Hope For Today'
- https://www.drugs.com/buprenorphine.html
- www.chatgpt.com

*Available worldwide from Amazon
and all good bookstores*

www.mtp.agency

www.facebook.com/mtp.agency

@mtp_agency

www.ingramcontent.com/pod-product-compliance
Lightning Source LLC
LaVergne TN
LVHW041639060526
838200LV00040B/1628